ROBERT J. KOZAK

GEORGE KRAFCISIN

A GUIDE TO ALIGNMENT AND INTEGRATION

QUALITY RESOURCES.
A Division of The Kraus Organization Limited
New York, New York

Most Quality Resources books are available at quantity discounts when purchased in bulk. For more information contact:
Special Sales Department
Quality Resources
A Division of The Kraus Organization Limited
902 Broadway
New York, New York 10010
800-247-8519

Printed in the United States of America

00 99 98 97 10 9 8 7 6 5 4 3 2 1

Quality Resources
A Division of The Kraus Organization Limited
902 Broadway
New York, New York 10010
212-979-8600
800-247-8519

The paper used in this publication meets the minimum requirements of American National Standard for Information Sciences—Permanence of Paper for Printed Library Materials, ANSI Z39.48-1984.

ISBN 0-527-76317-9

Library of Congress Cataloging-in-Publication Data

Kozak, Robert J.
Safety Management and ISO 9000/QS-9000 : a guide to alignment and integration / by Robert J. Kozak and George Krafcisin.
p. cm.
Includes bibliographical references and index.
ISBN 0-527-76317-9
1. Product safety—Management. 2. Industrial safety—Management. 3. ISO 9000 Series Standards. 4. QS-9000 (Standard) I. Krafcisin, George. II. Title.
TS175.K68 1996 96-41895
658.5'6—dc20 CIP

III

CONTENTS

III

ACKNOWLEDGMENTS

No book is ever written without outside help. We would like to thank the following people who provided insight, advice, and the experience of the real world: Roger Boyink, Chuck Brehm, Joel Charm, David B. Crawford, Chuck Heindrichs, Brian Lawrence, Marc Majewski, Ruth Trotman, and Rick Wrobel. Of course, any mistakes we made remain entirely ours.

We would also like to thank our editor, Cindy Tokumitsu, for guiding us through the process with patience, and our illustrator, Willem Mineur, for his clear artwork.

Last but not least, our thanks to Mary Beth, Rachel, Luke, Audrey, and Bev for their patience and support.

Bob Kozak and George Krafcisin

III

CHAPTER ONE

WHY USE THIS BOOK?

In 1995, *Industrial Hygiene and Safety News* conducted a survey of safety and health professionals. More than half of the small-plant, safety-program managers surveyed felt that improving employee safety behaviors and attitudes and "getting away from a compliance focus" will be of great importance in the next year and in the future. The problem is that almost 90 percent of the respondents felt that the size of their staff available to attack these problems would stay the same or decrease. How is the job going to get done?

America is experiencing global competition, and anyone who works for a major industry has seen the effect. We can no longer afford to have a staff of specialists to address all the things that need to be done. If you work for a small company, you may rely on outside expertise to address them. In large corporations, corporate- and division-level experts are gone. As a result, if an activity really needs to be done, it may get done by someone who wears several hats.

The new management paradigm is one of empowerment and efficiency. Small teams of workers on the front line make operating decisions. But they still need some kind of system to give them guidance. Not all workers have the vision to prioritize their work without a clear statement of what is to be done, what is important, and how to do it. There is always the need for specialized knowledge to fill in the gaps.

Product safety and occupational safety and health are examples of specialty fields in which the modern manager and worker need help. What place does safety hold in the priorities of the organization? Where does the manager turn to get the information needed to implement a system that will work? From where is the time to come, given that this manager also is responsible for production, security, fire protection, personnel, and other miscellaneous duties? Last, the most difficult problem—Where to start?

One organizational approach that can help is offered by the ISO 9000 quality management system standards and the automotive industry supplement, QS-9000 (for convenience, we will use the abbreviation "ISO/QS-9000" to refer to both systems). Your company has probably decided to become registered in one of the quality system standards. Why not use that experience to enhance the management of safety for workers and products? When safety becomes part of a company's culture, then safety becomes an integrated design philosophy.

If your company is in the process of ISO/QS-9000 certification, you will be happy to know that the effort you are making and the system you are building can help in safety. Effective safety and health programs are management systems with noticeable similarities to quality systems. Both quality and safety management programs succeed by involving all employees in the process. By using the same philosophy and framework you apply to your ISO or QS-9000 system, you can have a more effective program to help manage the safety of your product and your employees. You can also save the time involved in training workers in yet another management system.

This book presents approaches to building the framework for product safety and worker safety and health programs—the details are still up to you. But we believe that the program you build will be easier to implement and maintain, and probably more effective, if you follow the process framed by the ISO/QS-9000 quality management system standards.

If you do choose this path, you will be in step with trends in the safety and health arena. As we write this book, the safety and health community is preparing to follow the success of the ISO/QS-9000 paradigm. Professionals around the world are developing standards that use the quality management system approach to build effective safety and health systems. The Occupational Safety and Health Administration (OSHA) has formed a working group to develop a safety management program standard that may include incentives for voluntary compliance. Several states have developed similar programs. ISO itself is examining the need for a management system standard for occupational health and safety. And the ISO 14000 environmental management system standard, which is near final approval, is clearly adaptable to the management of occupational health and safety as well as environmental exposures.

Every program must be adapted to the specific needs of an organization. In this book we have outlined an approach to a program and given examples of how safety and health relate to the ISO/QS-9000 standards. We have included reference materials in the appendices so you can get the specific program guidance you need to fill in the details of your program. We hope this will be the start of a successful effort to integrate and/or align your quality and safety programs to make both of them more effective.

Our goal is to encourage industry to provide its customers and employees with safer products and a safer workplace by understanding and using the ISO/QS-9000 management system standards. We hope that this book will help safety and quality managers, engineers, production managers, auditors, government regulators, academicians, and other professionals involved in ISO/QS-9000 initiatives to expand their expertise and their contribution to their organizations.

III

CHAPTER 2

THE LINK BETWEEN QUALITY AND SAFETY

The Roots of Quality

Quality is defined in the ISO/QS-9000 system as the satisfaction of customer expectations. The requirements of ISO/QS-9000 are aimed primarily at achieving customer satisfaction by preventing nonconformity at all stages from design to servicing. One of the things customers expect, although they may not say so explicitly, is safety. For example, if you as a consumer buy a TV, you expect that it will do a number of things: It will receive the standard broadcast band as required by regulation. It will deliver the signal with volume and clarity commensurate with its price. It will work without malfunction at least through the warranty period. You also assume it will not give you an electric shock, catch fire, or have sharp parts or edges that could cause injury. Safety has become such an integral part of the quality of products that consumers assume that safety has been designed into the product and process from the start.

In the United States this assumption of safety has been so ingrained that lawsuits are filed for injuries and property damage that sometime seem only remotely connected to the product or service provided. Perhaps this is partly the result of a public attitude that business can afford to pay for injuries, partly the result of our legal system, and partly a feeling that someone else should surely pay for our misfortunes. We have all heard stories about extreme examples:

- A ladder manufacturer was sued for the injuries incurred when a customer placed the ladder on a pile of ice—when the ice thawed, the ladder fell over. Doesn't common sense dictate that one uses a ladder with the footing in mind?
- While driving, a customer of a fast-food chain spilled the cup of hot coffee she had placed between her legs. The company paid for the medical costs, pain and suffering, and punitive damages.
- An airplane manufacturer was sued for faulty manufacture when the light plane it made more than 20 years earlier crashed while trying to land in a storm. The pilot was allegedly under the influence of alcohol.

The actual product "quality"—does the product do what the customer expects?—is often not a factor in these cases. Indeed, in the coffee case, the temperature of the coffee was a customer-determined product specification: The company had determined that customers liked their coffee to be served at 190°F. In quality system terms, delivering cooler coffee might have been a process nonconformance.

These kind of stories make headlines because of their apparent unfairness. However, headlines are not often made when the quality of the product actually *was* a significant factor in the injury. These types of cases illustrate the importance of product safety:

- Several separate claims were filed against a manufacturer for falls and injuries incurred when its product did indeed break under normal use. Investigation showed that the product did not pass the most fundamental tests prescribed under the appropriate standard, and the quality system did not detect and prevent the nonconformance.

- A helicopter crash in Missouri resulted in two verdicts, one for $350 million and the other for $70 million. The manufacturer admitted in court that it had continued to use a dangerous engine component to save money.
- The parents of a child with cerebral palsy sued a New York hospital and won $45.3 million. The baby had suffered cardiac arrest, and due to equipment failure, was deprived of oxygen for 10 minutes.

Product safety is indeed an important issue.

Product Safety and ISO 9000

ISO 9000 is about product and service quality. The ISO 9000 standards do not replace the detailed product safety standards, codes, and/or regulations for products. Instead, the standards aim to assure that the products will be manufactured under a system that will take these detailed specifications as customer requirements, and that the requirements will be met or exceeded in a consistent fashion.

Some of the requirements are regulatory. Government regulation at the city, county, state, or federal level is such an integral part of the business environment that ignorance of its existence can lead to failure. A vital part of the ISO 9000 process is to first identify legal and regulatory aspects of your business, to minimize risk, and to ultimately provide customer satisfaction. Shigeo Shingo, the Japanese scientist, tells us, "The greatest waste is waste we don't see." If an ISO or QS-9000 system is implemented without due care for external regulations, costs and losses from violations may prove to be disastrous. For example, if you want to manufacture a new type of battery and aren't aware that county regulations would automatically ban its production because of one of its chemical ingredients, you are courting disaster. In fact, if we look at definitions for quality as issued by ISO, we can see that safety is embedded in the standards for product and service quality (see Figure 2.1).

Figure 2.1
ISO 8402: Quality Management and Quality Assurance Vocabulary

2.1 Quality—totality of characteristics of an entity that bear on its ability to satisfy stated and implied needs.

Notes: 1. In a contractual environment, or in a regulated environment, such as the nuclear safety field, needs are specified, whereas in other environments, implied needs should be identified and defined....

2.8 Safety—state in which the harm (to persons) or damage is limited to an acceptable level.

Notes: 1. Safety is one of the aspects of quality. 2. The above definition is valid for the purposes of quality standards. The term *safety* is defined in *ISO/IEC Guide 2.*

2.10 Nonconformity—nonfulfillment of a specified requirement.

2.11 Defect—nonfulfillment of an intended usage requirement of reasonable expectation, including one connected with safety....

2.12 Product Liability—generic term used to describe the onus on a user or others to make restitution for loss related to personal injury, property damage, or other harm caused by a product....

3.7 Total Quality Management—management approach of an organization centered on quality, based on the participation of all its members, and aimed at long-term success through customer satisfaction and benefiting all members of the organization and society.

ISO/IEC Guide 2

2.5 Safety—freedom from unacceptable risk of harm.

Source: ISO 8402 (rev. 1994), *Quality Management and Quality Assurance–Vocabulary.* (International Organization for Standardization)

Product Safety, Liability Prevention, and ISO/QS-9000

Historically, product specifications, codes, and regulations by themselves have not proven adequate in protecting the consumer. Dangerous, defective, and nonconforming consumer products take a large toll on our nation. More children die in the United States from accidental injuries than from disease. Each year there are 21,400 deaths and 29 million injuries related to consumer products. Deaths, injuries, and property damage from consumer products cost the United States about $200 billion annually, according to the U.S. Consumer Product Safety Commission (CPSC).

A summary of consumer products and associated injuries compiled by the National Safety Council and published in *1995 Accident Facts* is shown in Table 2.1.

Table 2.1
1995 Accident Facts

Product Type	Number of Injuries	Voluntary Safety Standards
Stairs, ramps, floors	1,879,029	ANSI A1264.1, UL77, FPA253, NSF529
Bicycles, accessories	649,536	ANSI Z315.1, SAE J 1451
Chairs, sofas	413,759	ANSI/BIFMA X5.1, ANSI/UL 964
Cutlery, knives	468,567	ANSI B94.31
Tables	345,271	ANSI/NSF 30, NFPA
Cans, containers	239,521	ANSI/UL 30, 32, MH 2, ASTM D2561, NFPA327
Playground equipment	290,382	ASTM F1148, AWPA C 17
Doors	357,152	ANSI/ BHMA156.8

The above table was selected from the U.S. National Electronics Injury Surveillance System (NEISS) report. The NEISS estimates are calculated from a statistically representative sample in the United States. Injury totals represent estimates of the number of treated hospital emergency room cases associated with various products. The product involved is not necessarily the cause of the accident.

Voluntary safety standards typically applicable to these products are shown in the far right column. Use of standards can yield positive results, according to CPSC reports (*Regulatory Reform Summary*, June 1995):

- Electrocution deaths were reduced 62%, from 650 to 250.
- Fire deaths were reduced 30%, from 5,450 to 3,800.
- Chain-saw injuries were reduced 48%, from 69,000 to 36,000.

A recent insurance company study of 27 random cases with product liability settlements larger than $100,000 showed the largest category of cause was related to design control. (This is directly treated by ISO/QS element 4.4. We will discuss the subject further in Chapter 5.)

Because our society appears to put little responsibility on consumers for their own conduct, it becomes necessary for industry to adopt maximum efforts to design safe products and promote their safe use. ISO/QS-9000 requires firms to design, manufacture, and deliver safe goods. Responsible companies

Figure 2.2
A Study on the Causes of Product Liability

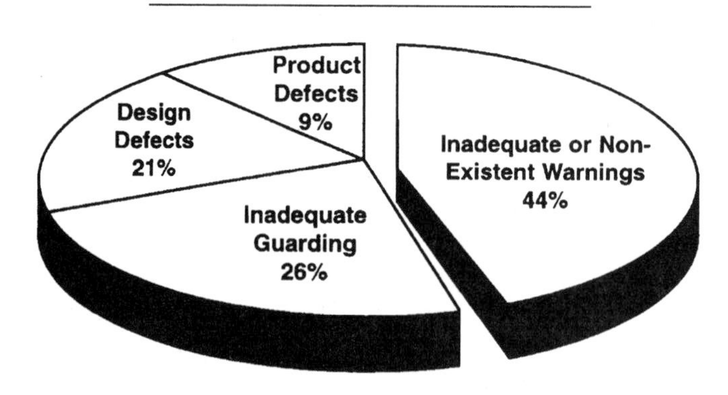

Source: *Quality Digest,* October 1995. Reprinted with permission from *Quality Digest.*

educate their customers on product safety, they market safety, and they realize that "safety sells" is more than a trend.

In addition to government regulation, consumerism has emerged as a potent market force. Consumer groups such as the Consumer Federation of America, the Consumers Union, Public Citizen, and National Safe Kids have published numerous reports on product safety. Educated consumers increasingly rely on these and other publications for their buying decisions.

Making products safe must be viewed not only as good business, but as the only way to do business. In March 1995, the CPSC hosted a "Safety Sells" Conference to talk about business profitability and safety as mutual objectives. Many senior executives spoke about their firms' new and creative strategies for making and selling safer products. Several of their comments are referenced here and in later chapters.

Michael Goldstein, vice chairman and chief executive officer of Toys "R" Us, says, "By having comprehensive safety assurance programs in place, we have reduced our internal operating costs involved with recalls. Furthermore, we have improved our customer service by making sure that only 'safe' toys are being sold in our stores."

Albert Dowden, president and chief executive officer of Volvo North America, with regard to Volvo's side-impact protection system says, "To put this issue into context, I first need to talk about how Volvo thinks about safety. Here is the central idea I want to leave you with: Safety doesn't result from devices. Putting an airbag in a tin box doesn't make a safe car. After all, the airbag may function perfectly, but that is scant protection if the engine is in your lap. Safety results from an overall approach to product conception, design, and construction.... While I am proud of the work we have done with our side-impact protection system, it's important to recognize that safety can only emerge from a total-design orientation. The public is increasingly attuned to safety as an essential attribute of the desirable car. Our strength at Volvo is not measured in the safety of individual features but in the safety of the overall product." See Figure 2.3.

Figure 2.3
Car Buyer's Safety Bill of Rights

Whereas motor vehicle crashes are the leading cause of death and disabling injury for children and young adults, result in 40,000 deaths and hundreds of thousands of serious injuries annually, and cost the Americans public over $137 billion every year, we the undersigned organizations believe American consumers buying a new motor vehicle for personal use have the right to:

1) Safe vehicles that can withstand most severe, real-world crashes with no serious injuries to the occupants;
2) Safety performance standards based on available and advanced technology to protect against rollover, occupant ejection, head impact, and costly crash incidents that cause severe injury and death;
3) Clear and useful information based on minimum crash test criteria for front, side, rear, and rollover crashes on every vehicle label and in the owner's manual;
4) Consumer information that augments—not replaces—effective motor vehicle safety standards;
5) A choice of vehicle types, features, and options in a variety of price ranges; and
6) Effective enforcement of safety standards, including prompt recall and repair of safety defects.

Advocates for Highway and Auto Safety
Alliance of American Insurers
American College of Preventive Medicine
American Insurance Association
American Public Health Association
Center for Auto Safety
Citizens for Reliable and Safe Highways
Consumer Federation of America
GEICO
Kemper National Insurance
Motor Voters
National Association of Developmental Disabilities Council
National Association of Pediatric Nurse Associates and Practitioners
National Safe Kids Campaign
Nationwide Insurance Enterprise
Progressive Insurance
Public Citizen
State Farm Insurance Companies
Trauma Foundation
U.S. Public Interest Research Group

Source: *The Safety Advocate*, Vol. 6, Nos. 1-2, Spring/Summer 1995. Reprinted with permission of Advocates for Highway and Auto Safety.

The CPSC has a mandate to "protect the public against unreasonable risks of injuries and deaths associated with consumer products." To get an idea of the CPSC's reach, visualize everything in a large shopping mall: Except for guns, drugs, tobacco, food, vehicles, and boats, the safety of nearly every item in the mall falls within the CPSC's scope. Estimates of the number of product categories covered range from 10,000 to 15,000.

Companies are required by law (16 CFR Part 1100 to 1406, Consumer Product Safety Act) to report substantial product hazards if:

- They receive information that a product fails to meet a product safety standard or regulation.
- A product has a defect or otherwise could create a substantial risk of injury.
- A product is the subject of at least three federal or state civil actions that allege the involvement of that product in death or grievous injury cases.

This requirement is similar to the requirements of the automotive industry and the medical-device industry for reporting to the National Highway Traffic Safety Administration (NHTSA) and the Food and Drug Administration (FDA), respectively.

The CPSC also has initiated a program to recognize substantial contributions to product safety. Several recent awards went to:

- Procter & Gamble for senior-friendly, child-resistant packaging.
- Playskool for passive restraints for high chairs.
- Sunbeam Plastics for senior-friendly, child-resistant packaging.
- Toy "R" Us for product safety programs.
- Whirlpool for outstanding commitment to consumer safety.

Factors that are considered in the awards process include:

- Actions that contribute to reducing the hazards to children and other vulnerable populations.
- Voluntary actions that are not mandated or go beyond government regulations.
- Developments that affect large numbers of individuals.
- Innovations or improvements to existing products.
- Safety devices, packaging, warnings, or products that enhance product safety.

These companies provide excellent examples for a progressive approach to product safety. We will encounter them later in Chapter 5 as we explore some of the details of an ISO and QS-9000–based product safety system.

Product Safety and Liability

It is the end-use customer that provides revenue for your company. That customer expects and deserves safe and reliable products. If your customer is injured or killed while using your company's product, a lawsuit may follow. Allegations of negligence in design, manufacture, and distribution, lack of essential information, and an unreasonably dangerous product are all possibilities. It will be up to your company to prove that a safe and reliable product was manufactured. Will the jury consider your company's product reasonably safe, or not unreasonably dangerous? How will the plaintiff's attorney demonstrate the reverse to the jury? How will your defense attorney counter?

Keep in mind that although ISO or QS-9000 registration is not a complete defense to any product liability claim, the 9000 standards may help in defense. Readers should pay close attention to ISO 9004-1, Quality management and quality systems elements, from a legal point of view. Although ISO 9004-1 is a voluntary standard, it does contain an entire element (19, Product Safety) describing product safety within an ISO/QS-9000–based management system. The U.S.

justice system has established manufacturers' "duty of care" to include voluntary standards. It is possible that in the future the courts may decide that ISO 9004-1 sets forth a standard for the conduct of a safe and prudent firm. In addition, product safety, product liability, and regulatory requirements are cited numerous times in ISO 9000-2, Quality management and quality assurance standards, Part 2—Guidelines for the application of ISO 9001, ISO 9002, and ISO 9003.

Although some elements of ISO/QS-9001 relate directly to product safety, and others less so, a fully implemented quality system that meets *all* ISO 9001 or 9002 requirements is essential to provide evidence for adequate defense in litigation. For example, if corrective action was not taken on test failures, or if required records were not retained, or if process controls were not in place, these all become a basis for showing a less than thorough product safety effort.

One way to address product safety and liability issues is to develop a safety and liability prevention program that corresponds to guidance set forth in ISO 9004-1 and ISO 9000-2 as well as the ISO/QS-9001, ISO 9002, and ISO 9003 requirements. Embed product safety and product liability prevention in your quality manual, procedures, and training programs. Study the applications chapters for element-specific issues that may apply to your type of industry. Remember, no matter what type of product you sell or manufacture, product safety is an issue. See Appendix A for a list of some product safety laws and regulations.

Occupational Safety and ISO/QS-9000

The management systems specified in ISO/QS-9000 are for the management of *people*—the workers that produce the products and deliver the services. Without even considering the moral obligation for providing a safe and healthy work environment for employees, an assumption that will not even be questioned here, no organization can function efficiently when accidents and injuries occur in the workplace. Many sections of ISO/QS-9000 refer specifically to considerations that are essential to the quality of the finished product or service and can also impact safety and health. The definition of total quality management given in ISO 8402 says that the system should ensure benefits to "all members of the organization." ISO 9004-1 defines the requirements of society as including "protection of the environment, health, safety, security..." (ISO 9004-1 3.3, Note 6).

In our opinion, if an organization chooses to consider safety as an integral part of the ISO standards, it will be in harmony with the intent of the standards.

Progress in Occupational Safety

As Note 1 to the ISO definition of quality states, the need for product safety may be specified or it may need to "be identified and defined." There are both regulatory and market drivers that make this identification necessary. The link between product safety and quality is clear. But the link between occupational safety and quality may not be quite so obvious.

There have always been hazards in the workplace. There are historical and artistic references to the hazards of work going back to early Roman times. But not until the industrial revolution in the nineteenth century and the early years of the twentieth did society decide that there was something fundamentally wrong with this system. Injured workers had to prove the negligence of their employer in order to receive compensation for an injury resulting from their job. If they did so and lost, assuming they had the money to pursue a suit, they ran the risk of losing their job.

In England and the United States, the beginning of the twentieth century saw the passage of legislation making the employer responsible for providing a safer place to work. Workers' Compensation laws in most of the states made an injury sustained in the course of work automatically compensable by the employer—a "no-fault" liability system. Workers did not have to prove negligence, but they waived their right to sue the employer for further compensation than that provided by the statutes. Workers' Compensation systems gave an economic incentive to employers to reduce the number of workplace injuries.

Unfortunately, when the decision to implement a safety program is made on economic grounds, the investment in safety becomes a matter of dollars and cents rather than a judgment of the best way to manage the process of making quality goods and offering quality services.

Safety professionals have spent considerable time trying to prove to management that the cost of injuries and accidents is much more than the direct cost paid in Workers' Compensation claims. The cost to the employer from disruption of the work process when an accident occurs is usually estimated at four to five times the direct cost of lost wages and medical expenses. When an accident occurs, workers stop to assist, equipment may be damaged, management must devote efforts to help the injured worker, and investigation of the accident occurs. If the worker cannot return to the job immediately, a new worker must be trained for the job, and production quality may suffer during the training period. An entire system of insurance, training, medical support, and administration must be maintained to take care of the injuries and damage that occur from accidents in the workplace. The National Safety Council estimates that the true cost of injuries and accidents in the workplace was over $120 billion in 1994. This amounts to almost $1,000 per worker.

Despite the economic arguments, companies made little progress in workplace accident reduction into the mid-century. Although the conditions that might result in accidents and illnesses were fairly well known by the 1960s, companies were often uninterested in doing anything about them. When one of the authors began work as an insurance company industrial hygienist in the mid-1960s, free consultation was provided to Workers' Compensation policyholders. When scheduling appointments to measure noise exposures to workers in industry, the response heard was often, "Why do you want to do that?" The long-term economic costs of hearing loss from noise exposure were too far in the future and too speculative to generate major efforts to reduce the hazard. (And in fact, Workers' Compensation payments for hearing loss generally result in only a fraction of a percent of the total bill for occupational injuries. Claims usually occur in cases of plant closings when large numbers of claims are filed simultaneously by laid-off workers.)

The lack of progress in safety resulted in Congress passing the Walsh-Healy Act in 1968. The act provided safety standards that were to be followed by all companies that provided goods and services under federal contracts. This act was the predecessor to the Occupational Safety and Health Act, which established OSHA, the Occupational Safety and Health Administration, as part of the Department of Labor. The Occupational Safety and Health Act of 1970 was designed "to assure so far as possible every working man and woman in the Nation safe and healthful working conditions and to preserve our human resources."

OSHA issues standards and rules for safe and healthful working conditions, tools, equipment, facilities, and processes. To set up the original standards, OSHA not only wrote its own, but adopted a number of established consensus standards developed by organizations such as the American National Standards Institute (ANSI) and the National Fire Protection Association (NFPA). OSHA also conducts workplace inspections to assure the standards are followed. The act and the standards apply to every private employer with one or more employees (except those covered by other federal legislation such as the Atomic Energy Act and the Coal Mine Safety Act). OSHA covers about 56 million employees at 3.6 million workplaces; states and territories that administer their own approved OSHA programs cover an additional 37 million employees at 2.4 million work sites.

Under the act, employers have the general duty of providing a workplace free from recognized hazards to safety and health, and they must comply with OSHA standards.

OSHA quickly became targeted by business as the most disliked government agency (perhaps second only to the IRS). The original OSHA standards contained a myriad of specification standards that many people felt had nothing to do with workplace safety. For example, one standard requiring split seats in toilet stalls was quickly used to ridicule the entire effort. However, most of the standards are important to worker safety and health. See Table 2.2.

Table 2.2
OSHA Federal Standard Violations:
29 CFR 1910 General Industry for Fiscal Year 1993

Sub-part	Standard	Sections	# of Violations	% of Total	Cumulative %
Z	Toxic & Hazardous Substances	.1000 –.1500	25,530	24%	24%
O	Machinery and Machine Guarding	.221–.222	15,780	15%	39%
S	Electrical	.301–.399	12,421	12%	51%
J	General Environmental Controls	.141–.150	9,357	9%	60%
H	Hazardous Materials	.101–.120	7,380	7%	67%
I	Personal Protective Equipment	.132–.140	6,011	6%	73%
D	Walking/Working Surfaces	.21–.32	5,588	5%	78%
E	Means of Egress	.35–.40	4,737	5%	83%
L	Fire Protection	.155–.165	3,488	3%	86%
N	Materials-handling	.176–.190	3,389	3%	89%
C	General Safety and Health	.20	3,004	3%	92%
G	Health and Environmental Controls	.94–.100	2,494	2%	94%
Q	Welding, Cutting, & Brazing	.251–.254	2,023	2%	96%
K	Medical and First Aid	.151–.153	1,700	2%	98%
P	Hand & Portable Power Tools	.241–.247	1,193	1%	99%
R	Special Industries	.261–.275	740	0%	100%
T	Commercial Diving	.401–.441	124	0%	100%
F	Powered Platforms	.66–.70	63	0%	100%
M	Compressed Gas	.166–.171	46	0%	100%
TOTAL			105,068		

Contrast the statistics of Table 2.2 with the Bureau of Labor Statistics reports on the actual sources of occupational injuries shown in Table 2.3.

Table 2.3
Number of Nonfatal Occupational Injuries and Illnesses Involving Days Away from Work (1993)
(for all private industry, in thousands)

Source	
Floors, walkways, ground surfaces	340.2
Worker position or motion	332.0
Containers	330.3
Parts and materials	249.1
Vehicles	157.4
Machinery	154.1
Tools, instruments, and equipment	141.8
Health care patient	99.4
Furniture and fixtures	88.8
Chemicals	43.4
Event or Exposure	
Overexertion	635.8
Contact with objects and equipment	614.6
Overexertion in lifting	380.4
Struck by object	294.2
Fall to same level	244.1
Struck against object	161.8
Exposure to harmful substances	111.5
Fall to lower level	111.3
Caught in equipment or object	98.2
Repetitive motion	94.3
Slips, trips, loss of balance—w/o fall	83.1
Transportation accidents	71.3
Assaults and violent acts by person	21.3
Fires and explosions	4.8

One effect that the act had was to generate an incentive for industry to maintain safety and health professionals to ensure compliance. In companies with a philosophy of managing their operations to achieve the highest degree of safety and health for their workers, those professionals were able to develop and implement OSH programs that really reduced the incidence and severity of accidents and illnesses.

OSHA has resulted in an emphasis on, and improvement in, occupational safety and health. But OSHA has often been criticized on several counts:

- Many OSHA standards aim at controlling the physical aspects of the working environment, whereas most experts agree that the majority of accidents occur because of employee behavior.
- OSHA has traditionally focused on specification standards that aim at correcting detailed workplace conditions, rather than setting a performance goal of reducing accidents by the most appropriate and efficient means.
- OSHA has depended on "Command and Control": inspection, enforcement, and penalties for noncompliance. However, OSHA cannot possibly inspect all workplaces.
- Actual accident and injury rates have declined significantly in some specific industries and for certain exposures that OSHA has targeted. But problems still exist in industry in general and in areas where OSHA has been unable to concentrate resources.

OSHA itself recognizes these shortcomings of the traditional approach in its paper "The New OSHA—Reinventing Worker Safety and Health":

> *First, despite OSHA's efforts, every year over 6,000 Americans die from workplace injuries, an estimated 50,000 people die from illnesses caused by workplace chemical exposures, and 6 million people suffer nonfatal workplace injuries. Injuries alone cost the economy more than $110 billion a year. These numbers are too high, because many workplace injuries and illnesses are predictable*

and preventable. Workplaces must be encouraged to make breakthrough improvements in injury and illness rates.

Second, in the public's view, OSHA has been driven too often by numbers and rules, not by smart enforcement and results. Business complains about overzealous enforcement and burdensome rules. Many people see OSHA as an agency so enmeshed in its own red tape that it has lost sight of its own mission. And too often, a "one-size-fits-all" regulatory approach has treated conscientious employers no differently from those who put workers needlessly at risk.

Figure 2.4
Deaths in the Workplace, 1994
(Total = 6,588 Deaths)

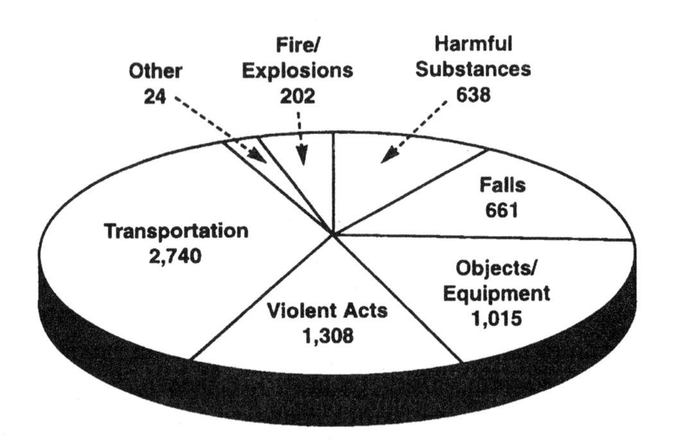

Source: Bureau of Labor Statistics

As a result, current thinking in OSHA and the safety community has been to look for a better way to motivate and help business reduce the number of occupational injuries and illnesses. Business should take advantage of this opportunity to set the tone of cooperation with government to replace the adversarial relationship of the past.

Safety Management Systems

Long before OSHA, the DuPont Company produced explosives. The extreme hazard of its product led it to establish safety as one of the essential elements of its management system: Its business would not succeed unless the inherent hazard of its product was controlled. The result of the management of occupational safety and health as an integral part of the business was a low incidence of accidents at DuPont. This success became the paradigm for safety management for industry. By the early 1980s, many companies had adopted the idea that managing safety and health for employees was identical to managing any other aspect of their business. Those companies achieved accident rates well below their industry averages.

For example, a textile manufacturer wanted to know why the safety performance of certain individual plants in the company was so different from almost identical operations in other locations. From interviews with employees from the chairman to the shop floor, it was clear that the safest plants were those where top management was held accountable for meeting safety performance objectives. Those objectives were given the same weight as production, cost, and customer service goals. In one case, a division vice president refused to give a net performance rating to one of his plant managers any higher than a "B"—his ranking for safety performance—even though the manager's ranking was an "A" for his financial and service objectives. The impact on the manager's bonus was substantial. The next year, his safety rating was an "A."

In another example, a division manager remembered his first order after a promotion to plant manager: The first lost-time accident would result in a meeting of the foreman, production manager, and safety coordinator in his office immediately after the accident, regardless of the time. The first meeting was at 2 a.m. after a third-shift accident. The next meeting did not occur for nearly two years, after more than a million work-hours of accident-free operation.

A major pharmaceutical and health care products manufacturer established its safety policy at the top management level. Its goal was to have the world's safest and healthiest workforce. The policy required the top manager of any facility worldwide to report in person before the top executive board within 48 hours of any severe accident—a fatality or amputation, for example. The lost-time injury rate for this company fell precipitously within four years, reaching the lowest rate in the industry. When this example was mentioned to a gathering of safety directors of another multinational company, one of them responded sadly, "We'd have to buy an airline to handle the traffic."

These examples seem familiar: Establish a policy that places safety as a specific organizational goal; hold managers accountable for the results; establish measurement systems that feed back into preventive measures. These are all part of the ISO 9000 management system as applied to product and service quality. In other words, the companies that have been successful in reducing workplace injuries and illnesses are companies that treat the safety of their employees in the same way they treat product quality. Safety is not just another thing you do when you have time; it's part of the whole business.

The current trend in companies that have achieved success in quality management and safety is to manage safety in a manner similar to the way they manage quality. In QS-9000, the automotive supplement to ISO 9000, for example, several sections refer directly to the safety of the working environment:

- 4.6.1 (Purchasing): "All materials used in part manufacture shall satisfy current governmental and safety constraints on restricted, toxic and hazardous materials; as well as environmental, electrical and electromagnetic considerations applicable to the country of manufacture and sale. ..."
- 4.9 (Process Control): "A supplier shall have a process to ensure compliance with all applicable government safety and environmental regulations. ..."
- 4.17 (Internal Quality Audits): "Suitable working environment shall be considered as part of the internal audit process."

- 2.3 (Techniques for Continuous Improvement): "The supplier shall demonstrate knowledge of the following measures and methodologies and shall use those that are appropriate... . Analysis of motion/ergonomics. ..."
- 3.1 (Facilities, Equipment, and Process Planning and Effectiveness): "Methods shall be developed for evaluating the effectiveness of existing operations and processes considering the following factors:... ergonomics and human factors. ..."

It should be noted that QS-9000 is specifically for automotive suppliers of production and service parts and materials, including processes such as plating and heat treatment. QS-9000 is much more prescriptive than ISO 9001. It spells out the details of *how* something is to be done, rather than describing only the outcome or objective of the standard. The goal for Quality System Requirements QS-9000 is the development of fundamental quality systems that provide for continuous improvement, emphasizing defect prevention and the reduction of variation and waste in the supply chain.

Given all of these common factors in standards, regulations, liability considerations, workplace safety, and management systems, the time is ripe for safety and health and product safety to become a part of the management system aligned with the drive for quality.

III

CHAPTER 3

CURRENT TRENDS IN ISO AND SAFETY

Things are changing fast in the area of occupational safety and health. ISO 14000 is near publication and several countries have proposed occupational health and safety standards. ISO is evaluating the need for an international standard for occupational safety and health management systems. You will want to stay current with the appropriate standards and regulations as they develop.

ISO 14000

In 1996, final approval was made for the ISO 14001 standard on environmental management systems. The ISO 14001 is intended to apply to environmental management systems. The introduction states, "This standard is not intended to address, and does not include requirements for aspects of occupational health and safety management; however it does not seek to discourage an organization from developing integration of such management system elements. Nevertheless the certification/registration process will only be applicable to the environmental management system aspects." It has been suggested that the standard can be used as a general framework for a safety and health program.

ISO 14001 contains the following headings:

- Environmental Policy must:
  - Be Appropriate to Operations;
  - Contain a Commitment to Continuous Improvement;
  - Ensure and Affirm Compliance with Regulations;
  - Establish a Framework for Setting Objectives;
  - Be Documented, Implemented, and Communicated to All Employees;
  - Be Available to the Public.
- Planning must:
  - Identify All Environmental Impacts of Operations;
  - Identify All Legal and Other Requirements;
  - Set Objectives and Targets;
  - Assign Responsibility and a Time Frame for the Environmental Management Program.
- Implementation and Operation must:
  - Give Authority, Resources, and Provide Structure and Responsibility;
  - Provide for Training, Awareness, Competence;
  - Establish Communication (Internal and External);
  - Provide for Documentation and Document Control;
  - Establish Operational Control (Procedures);
  - Provide for Emergency Preparedness.
- Checking and Corrective Action must:
  - Perform Monitoring and Measurement;
  - Address Nonconformance and Corrective and Preventive Action;
  - Keep Records;
  - Carry Out Environmental System Audit.
- Management Review

A table of corresponding paragraphs between ISO 14001 and ISO 9001 can be found in Appendix D. The ISO 14000 set of standards in its final form can serve as a template or framework for a safety and health program in itself. Some professionals have pointed out that the ISO 14000 format is more easily adapted than the ISO 9000 series as a template for safety and health programs. Companies like AlliedSignal, Texas Instruments, and Raychem have begun to develop systems combining environmental standards with safety and health and quality management systems.

When some experience is gained with the ISO 14000 standards, it would be well worth the effort to consider this approach to your program.

Future ISO Occupational Health and Safety Management System (OHSMS) Standards

In 1995, the ISO Technical Management Board called for a study of the need for an international standard for safety and health management systems. At the time of this publication, a meeting held by ANSI in the United States determined that the national position was not to favor ISO OHSMS standards. ISO recently held a similar meeting in Geneva; the majority of countries that took a formal position on the issue did not support an ISO standard, but there was general interest in and support for national guidelines.

There are a number of issues that need to be worked out before a standard is even considered. For example, because the issue of workplace safety and health involves both employers and workers, labor issues come up in the context of safety. How much involvement should workers have in managing the safety program? Are issues like working hours to be included in a standard? There is a lot of discussion left on the subject, but an international standard may be coming. If it is developed, there will be pressure to harmonize it with the existing ISO 9000 and ISO 14000 series of standards.

OSHA

Both the current Democratic administration and the Republican Congress are attacking OSHA in the name of reinventing government, fiscal reality, and decentralization. In OSHA's report on the topic, OSHA said it will "reinvent" 39 percent of the Code of Federal Regulations that apply to safety. Most of the revisions will come from 29 CFR 1910, the job safety and health regulations for general industry.

This is all a part of the "Reinventing OSHA" program that the agency announced in early 1995. The agency has an agenda that includes changing its approach from a philosophy of command and control and penalties for noncompliance to one of partnership with industry to reduce injuries. OSHA intends to reduce inspection rates and penalties for organizations that show a true commitment to safety and health through the implementation of an effective safety and health program. The other side of the coin is that organizations that have high incidence rates will be targeted for more frequent OSHA inspections. This has already resulted in the "Maine 200" approach, in which OSHA concentrated on 200 employers with 1,300 work sites in Maine (1 percent of the employers and 30 percent of the workforce) that account for 45 percent of Workers' Compensation injuries and illness. The program has already resulted in six of ten of the employers reducing their lost-time injury rates; Workers' Compensation claims are decreasing.

OSHA has also announced its program to develop a safety and health program standard. The effort is to begin in 1996. Details of the "Reinventing OSHA" program can be obtained from your local OSHA office or the sources listed in Appendix B.

On the Republican side of the aisle in Congress, a determined effort has been made to reduce OSHA's ability to set standards and inspect workplaces. The final outcome of the legislative battle is not clear, but it is certain that OSHA will have less money in the future and will be forced into reinventing itself and its approach to safety and health.

This presents an opportunity for industry to lower the incidence of accidents and injuries to workers, save money on accident costs, and avoid having OSHA showing up at the door to inspect. A good safety and health program can achieve all of these objectives. The ISO 9000 framework is a good place to start.

The States and OSHA

OSHA partners with 25 states to enforce regulations. Part of OSHA's new program includes a plan to allow states to try new and innovative programs to improve safety and health without necessarily following existing OSHA procedures and standards in lockstep.

Development of Sector-Specific Management Standards

The state of California has developed a safety and health standard, and the Australians, Irish, Dutch, and Norwegians have all launched proposals to develop them. The British standard, BS 8800, Occupational health and safety management systems, has been finalized. The French have adapted ISO 9002 and applied it to the road transportation of goods and dangerous substances in tanks.

Specific industry sectors have developed management system standards for their own special operations. For example, the ISO Technical Committee 67 on Materials, Equipment and Offshore Structures for Petroleum and Natural Gas Industries has prepared a draft standard entitled "Health, Safety, and Environmental Management Systems for Oil and Gas Production Operations and Facilities." The draft follows the format of ISO 14001.

The chemical industry has developed and implemented their "Responsible Care®" program. Compliance is a requirement for membership in the Chemical Manufacturers Association (CMA). Employee health and safety is one of the six codes of management practices contained in the program. The CMA is now investigating a system of third-party registration to the standard.

Many individual companies have established their own internal standards for safety and health. Some of these programs, such as those established by Johnson & Johnson,

Union Camp, and Raychem, follow the general philosophy of the ISO management system standards. IBM's Charlotte, North Carolina, facility modified and included its safety and health procedures in its ISO 9000 documentation.

The American Industrial Hygiene Association has developed a professional guidance document that will follow the ISO 9000 scheme.

It appears that there will be a number of ISO-type management system standards available to use.

III

CHAPTER 4

ISO 9000 AND YOUR WORKPLACE SAFETY PROGRAM

Integrating Management Systems

What does it mean to "integrate" safety into a quality management system? Very simply, the ISO 9000 series of standards is a set of management system standards. All management systems—organized methods of achieving a goal—have common aspects:

- Policy decisions that set the priority for the program
- Specified management responsibilities and objectives
- Documented processes that define responsibilities
- Document control
- Input from laws, customers, hazard analysis, and standards that determine the design of the output
- Control of essential/important operations
- Control of system inputs (raw materials)
- Training of workers
- Auditing of the system
- Testing of the output

- Corrective and preventive actions that feed back to the policy and organization

Figure 4.1 shows a flow chart of a typical management system.

Figure 4.1
Flow Chart of Management Systems

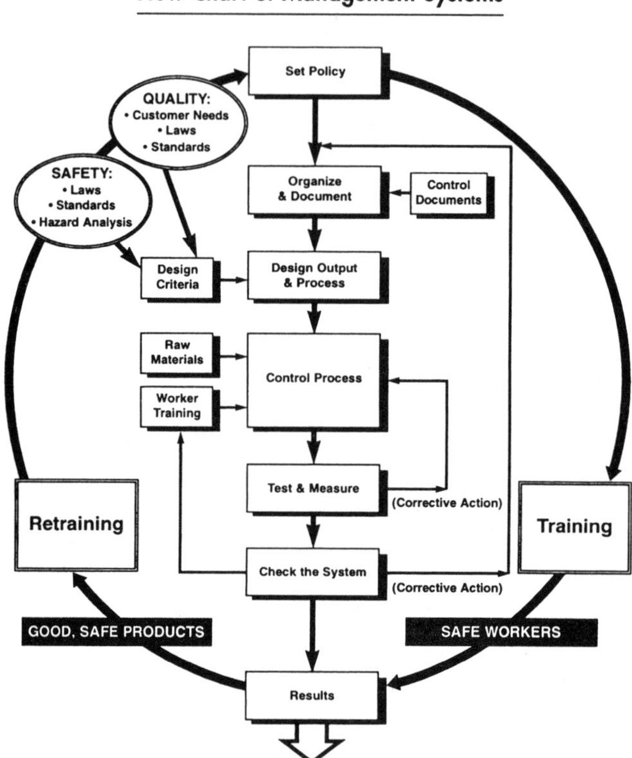

In this book, *integration* means applying these basic concepts to organizational systems that have different goals. For example, both quality and safety systems aim at improving performance in two different areas: Consistency in the quality of the product in the first case, and safety of employees in the second. However, both systems use common elements to achieve those goals: They both need documented procedures directed toward set objectives, control of documents, corrective action systems, etc. Thus, the same general management processes can direct activities of the people in an organization to achieve different goals that have been determined to be important. Of course, the detailed procedures required to accomplish the objectives of the two systems remain different; but they are set up, carried out, measured, and controlled in the same manner.

Why is it important to integrate these systems? There are several reasons:

- Isolated management systems in an organization create confusion and complexity as workers stop to think, "Which procedures manual was I supposed to use here?"
- All organizations start and finish their management processes at the same points: Top management sets priorities, and they are carried out at the production level by employees.
- Eliminating redundant systems reduces costs (one record keeping system, for example).
- Uniform systems are easier to coordinate.
- All people in the organization find it easier to understand the system.
- Finally, the quality systems standards have been very successful in getting management to commit resources to training and implementing them. Why not take advantage of this success?

Here are three comments addressing different aspects of the issue:

"We can't continue to think about management systems in silos; we must find a way to integrate them," said Joel Charm, director of occupational health and safety for AlliedSignal Corp., and chairman of the U.S. Technical Advisory Group to ISO/Technical Committee 207 for Subcommittee 1.

Hans Dieter Seghezzi, president of the Swiss Committee for Testing and Certification and vice president of the Swiss

Federal Commission for Accreditation, agrees that standards should be integrated. "A company needs one management system that builds on itself. Companies with a bunch of different systems that overlap will be in big trouble," he said.

In spite of the good intentions demonstrated by many parties, there is a real threat that the integration of management systems will be hampered. A study carried out at the instigation of Professor Waszink, holder of the RvA/Chair at Erasmus University of Rotterdam, showed that a wrong approach may lead to high expenses. (RvA Annual Report, 1994)

Figure 4.2 shows the interelationships of management functions in an integrated system.

Figure 4.2
Ball Bearing Model Illustrating Integrated Systems

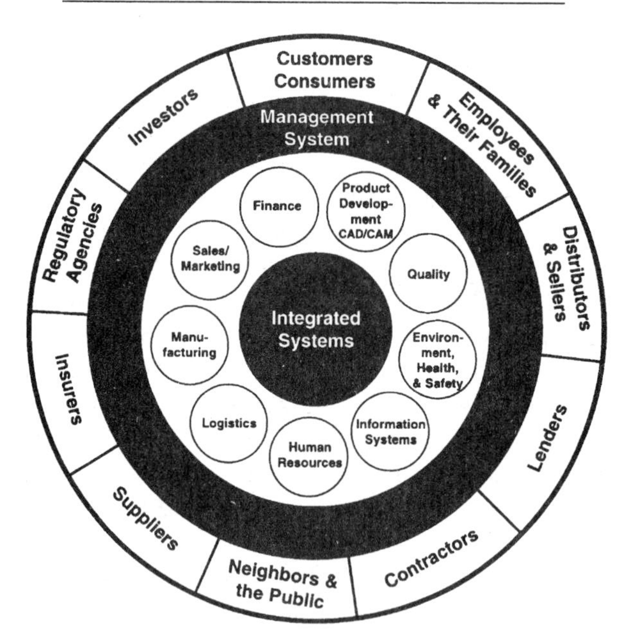

Source: Adapted from RvA 1994 Annual Report.

This chapter offers guidance toward applying the framework of the ISO 9000 quality management system standards to your safety and health program. The intent is to give practical suggestions to promote a better and more unified management system regardless of the approach used. Each element of the ISO 9001 standard is listed with an italicized paraphrase of what that element covers. QS-9000 follows this exactly. This is followed by a section with some elements of a safety and health program that may fit the ISO 9001 element. A final section describes typical safety and health "noncompliances" that are often seen in industry and that might be found in an audit of the program conducted by your own staff or by a third party. These guidelines are not meant to be all-inclusive, but are presented to help you start to integrate your own safety and health management system into the ISO and QS-9000 quality management system.

Many companies have integrated their safety and health programs into their quality program by actually including some safety procedures in the quality program documentation and procedures. See Figure 4.3 for an example of the management paradigm, "Plan, Do, Check, Act," applied to EHS Affairs. For example, where the quality program manual contains a procedure for calibration of test equipment, it will list safety testing equipment as well. Or, work instructions for process control will include safety precautions and procedures. Some programs insert none of the actual safety and health program elements into the quality program procedures and documents; some include almost all the elements. For example, if a company is already ISO 9001 registered, and seeks to integrate safety and health into its ISO 9001 system, it may choose to modify slightly the Tier I and Tier II documents (quality manual and procedures). It may also choose to add an element 21 to address the safety system requirements and bring the safety procedures into the system as a Tier III module. Another approach would be to develop a guide to show how existing separate quality, health and safety, and environmental system manuals interrelate. The order of precedence of the policies and procedures should be stated to clarify and coordinate among the many different functions in the company. The Dutch Council for Certification, Raad voor Accreditatie (RvA), an international accreditation body, has proposed requirements for registrars of environmental man-

Figure 4.3
Operating Model for Management of EHS Affairs

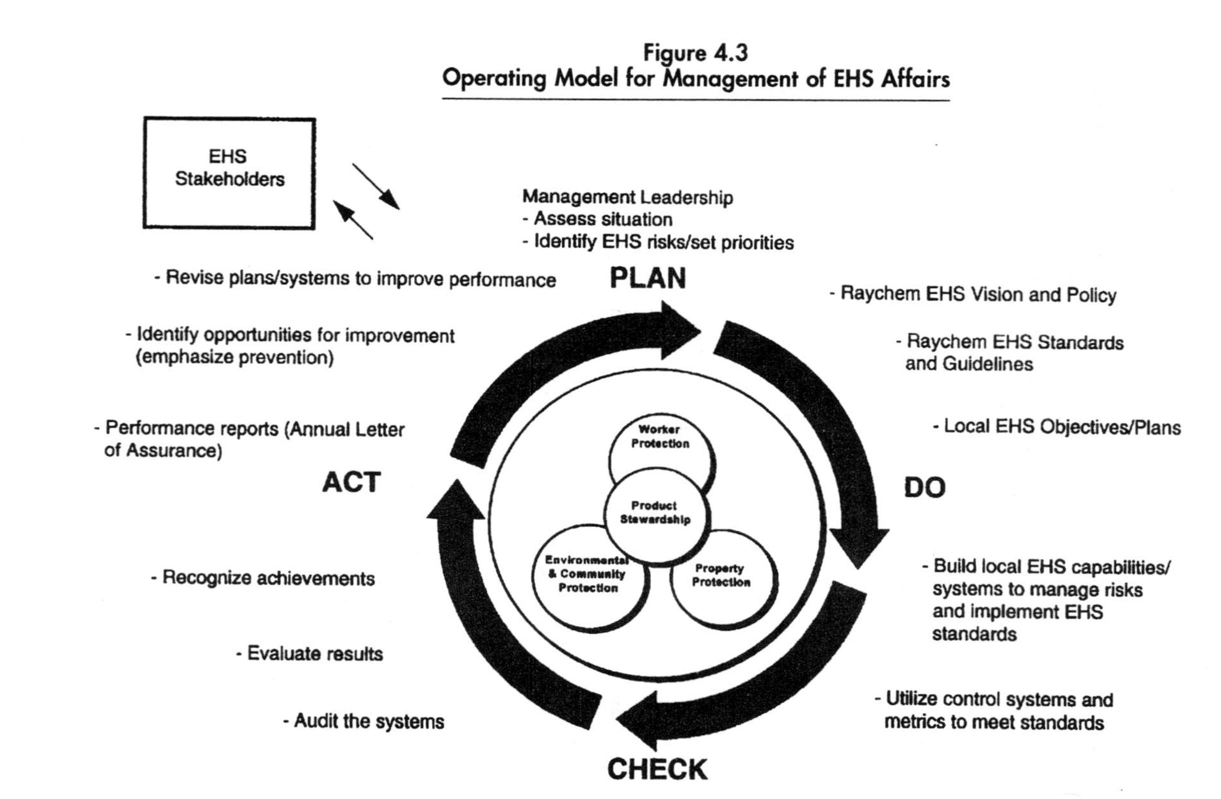

agement systems. One of the requirements is that the organization being audited must have a manual that makes clear the relationship of the environmental management system at the site to other management systems in use.

Several companies are saving time and money by combining policy development, goals and objectives, training, and corrective action requirements into a unified management system.

Most companies we have discussed this with have chosen to develop their safety and health programs in a *parallel* manner to the quality program. They use the same procedure format and language, the same general concepts, the same philosophy. They do not include all safety and health program elements directly in the documents of their ISO quality program, but some degree of direct integration always occurs. We call this approach *alignment.*

Combining the two systems so that the quality system *includes* the safety and health system has advantages and disadvantages. Using the same framework makes it easier for everyone to understand and use the program. But if the ISO and safety programs are integrated so that process instructions also contain safety program elements and procedures, the safety program may become an auditable portion of your ISO or QS-9000 system. You should discuss this with your registrar prior to the audit. Your registrar may audit a portion of the safety program to ensure compliance. For example, if a work instruction calls for a machine guarding inspection, the registrar may include machine guarding in the audit. This may possibly make it harder to achieve and maintain registration. You may also lack confidence in the ability of the auditor to audit a safety program.

Another disadvantage of integration is that some elements of good safety programs have to be "forced" to fit into the ISO 9000 scheme: Emergency preparedness, for example, does not directly correspond to any ISO quality standard element without stretching the concept of the standard beyond recognition. Safety requirements often include behavioral aspects that are not typically addressed in quality procedures. The ISO 9000 system also does not call for a baseline audit of hazards that are an essential part of a safety and health program (ISO 14001 for environmental management systems does require a baseline evaluation of environmental exposures). These parts of the program may need to reside "outside" the quality program. Trying to fit them into an existing quality system element may only be confusing.

A disadvantage of keeping the safety and quality programs separate, however, is that you will have two separate management systems to control. You may have more trouble maintaining the safety system if it requires yet another management system to keep track of.

What have some progressive companies done in this effort?

Actual Experience with Integrating ISO and Safety

In order to find what is already in use and working in the real world, the authors undertook a survey of companies that are both ISO 9000 registered *and* had Star status—the highest achievement category—in the OSHA Voluntary Protection Program (VPP). (See Appendix B for a description of the VPP.) The objective was to validate some of the concepts employed here and pass on the advice of these firms to our readers.

At the time of publication, there are 35 firms that achieved both the Star and ISO 9000 registration status. We talked to several of these companies both at the corporate and plant level. They are generally industry leaders in safety performance. The survey revealed that most of the firms have safety programs that are parallel to and linked with the ISO quality program. This means that separate programs were established with separate manuals and procedures, but because they use the same terminology, the same management system approach, and the same philosophy of continuous improvement, the safety and health programs are integrated with the quality systems. See Figure 4.4 for a description of Raychem's evolving EHS functions.

Varying numbers of safety and health program elements were actually incorporated into the quality system, but:

- 63 percent have some combination of separate development and various levels of system integration.

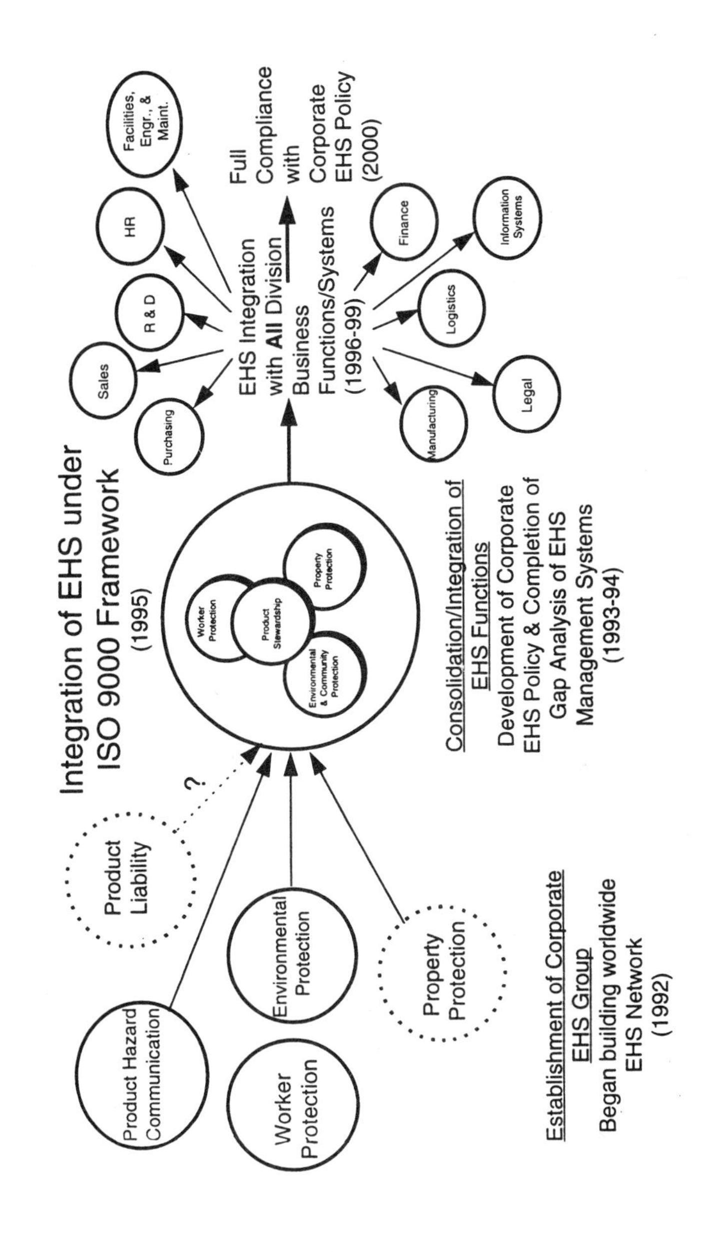

Figure 4.4
Raychem's Evolving EHS Function: Development of Corporate EHS Standards, Guidelines, and Policy Implementation Tools

- 25 percent of the firms run completely parallel and separate programs; there is no melding of the two systems.
- 12 percent have totally integrated systems in which safety and health procedures and programs were contained in the same system as the quality program. Thus, a work instruction would contain requirements for both product quality and safety.

The degree of integration or incorporation is up to you and the demands of your own situation; but some degree of parallel development, according to our survey, will reap benefits in your safety and health program.

Comments from the ISO 9000/VPP Star firms surveyed:

- "We did ISO first, now we are integrating safety."
- "Our ISO steering committee agreed to safety goals and to include the safety function in its membership."
- "We built our programs together from the start and integrated safety later. The safety and health function is included in all our ISO plant teams."
- "Make safety everyone's responsibility, using better procedures to enhance people's understanding of safety and compliance as it relates to their work."
- "Safety indirectly worked with quality using the Star program as guidance. Nothing was cut and paste, but the same framework applied."
- "All safety and health policies and program reviews are put into the same ISO document format."

Recommendations from the firms:

- It helps to start with one program and then develop the other. The great benefit is that all employees are involved in both programs.
- Stick with one program, ISO or safety and health, and finish it before doing the other. Also, a good safety committee is essential to do the detailed hazard analysis.

- A very active safety committee and employee-driven safety program made the integration process a success.
- Merge industrial hygiene controls, ergonomics, and the safety program with ISO 9000. Adopt safe work procedures for every process and include them in the ISO 9000 documentation.
- ISO 14000 will be our safety and health program. Procedures will be aligned so that they are "inextricably linked": Staff will use the same language and philosophy when writing and using procedures.
- We did the entire process in-house without consultants. This cost us some wasted efforts, but helped us learn more.

Pitfalls:

- Difficult getting everyone to buy into the process and understand, especially management.
- Not enough time to fully integrate programs and ensure that different departments have congruent goals.
- We are going to a "work cell" concept: An empowered team makes all the decisions. Safety and health may no longer exist as a staff function. Providing training for all these people will be a challenge.

Benefits:

- ISO 9000 discipline helped us to attain the STAR in VPP, especially on the documentation and keeping it up to date.
- Safety awareness is heightened. Also, we reduced accidents, lost time, and reduced Workers' Compensation costs.
- Customer complaints have dropped drastically. Safety awareness and employee involvement has greatly increased. No OSHA recordable injuries for two years.

- Star got us from an incident rate of 4.5 down to 3.0 compared to 10.0 or 12.0 for the industry. Workers' Compensation costs are also down considerably.
- We now have executive management buy-in for safety integrated elements, having first done ISO. Management is now comfortable with the investment.

In summary, experience with the two programs may help answer the following questions:

1. Should I attempt to integrate safety and health into the ISO program before, during, or after registration?

   Answer: Our respondents found it difficult to sustain the effort to do both programs at once. They recommend you finish one program and use the experience to build the other.

2. Will my registrar audit my safety and health program? Will that cost extra? Will it make attaining and maintaining registration more difficult?

   Answer: Before you become registered, discuss the issue of scope. If the registrar agrees to exclude the safety and health program from the quality system audit, there is no problem. However, if safety and health aspects are included in process and task procedures and work instructions, and are not followed, the registrar may issue a nonconformance to your system. Additional cost for auditing additional aspects of a management system should also be discussed with the registrar.

It is not expected that most registrars would perform in-depth audits of safety and health or other nonquality system items.

3. What role should safety and health professionals play in building the quality system?

   Answer: They should participate on all appropriate teams to be sure that occupational and product safety concerns are built into the system. The experience will also help in developing the safety and health system later.

A Suggested ISO 9000 Framework for Safety and Health

The following element-by-element approach gives a framework for building your safety and health program. It gives section-by-section examples of the safety program elements that may apply in your operations with the corresponding ISO/QS-9001 framework. This is only one suggested approach that may work in the context of your organization; you have the freedom to modify it as you please and as it works best. Please note that just as no one quality program will fit your specific organization, the details of your safety program will have to be customized.

A quality program is usually structured in a three-tiered fashion: The top level is a statement of policy, and establishes the structure of the entire program; the second level is a set of specific procedures that act as guides for carrying out the program; and the third is the work instructions used by workers to perform specific tasks. Accompanying the instructions may be various controlled forms and records that document the performance of the process.

As an example of the top level of a safety program, look at the OSHA Voluntary Protection Program (see Appendix B). That system is based on the following general policies (from OSHA Fact Sheet No. OSHA 9137):

- Management commitment and employee involvement
- Work-site analysis
- Hazard prevention and control
- Safety and health training

These concepts form a framework for a generally accepted safety and health program that can be adapted to fit your program. The following sections describe how some of the elements of a safety and health program can be placed within the framework of the ISO 9000 series of quality standards.

4.1 Management Responsibility

Define and document policy for quality, including objectives for quality and commitment to quality.

Guidelines for Safety Program Elements

- No management system works unless top management has assigned a priority to it and all employees understand it. Your program will need a clearly stated policy so that all personnel understand the priority of safety and health protection in relation to other organizational values. The system must set clear goals for the safety and health program and objectives for meeting that goal so that everyone understands the desired result and the measures planned for achieving it.
- Top management must be involved in implementing the program so that all employees will understand that the commitment is serious. Involvement means more than signing the policy and checking results at the end of the year: It means that a manager at the executive level is involved on a frequent basis in the operations of the safety program, and that executive-level meetings include safety as a regular agenda item.
- Because employee behavior affects safety experience as much as physical hazard conditions, all employees need to be involved in the structure and operation of the program and in decisions that affect their safety and health. This approach also makes full use of employees' insight and energy. The old style of safety program, in which management delegates all responsibility to the safety director, leads to employees forgetting about safety until the next meeting.
- Management must assign specific responsibilities for all aspects of the program to designated individuals. This makes it easier for managers, supervisors, and employees in all parts of the organization to know what performance is expected of them. Managers, supervisors, and

employees must be held accountable for meeting their responsibilities, so that essential tasks will be performed. They should have their safety duties and the results of those activities included in their performance reviews

- Management must provide adequate authority and resources to the responsible parties, so that their assigned responsibilities can be met.
- Top management must hold periodic reviews of the program to evaluate its success in meeting the established goal and objectives. Deficiencies should be identified and the program and/or the objectives revised when the goal and objectives are not met.

Typical Noncompliances in a Safety Program Audit

- Safety policy is posted in the lobby of a plant—but is obsolete and signed by a manager who has left the company.
- Top management established safety committees but appointed no executive-level "champion" to be a member. No executive attends safety committee meetings.
- The assignment of coordinator of safety is made to an individual who has so many other duties that no time is available to perform the safety function.
- Performance appraisals do not include the results of the safety program activities.
- No management reviews of the results of the safety program are conducted.

4.2 Quality System

Establish, maintain, and document the overall management system for quality, including procedures and work instructions.

Guidelines for Safety Program Elements

- Develop a manual that sets the format and formally documents in writing the safety and health policy, procedures, and work instructions. The manual may be organized in a tiered format, with the general policy at the top, and work procedures, instructions, and forms at lower levels.

- The manual should address all aspects of the safety and health program, and function as the directory of the program. In other words, if an outsider wants to know how the program addresses any aspect of safety and health, the manual would describe all levels, from policy to work instructions.
- Include all significant programs that will be part of the safety and health effort. This is the place to include items that are not normally considered as parallel to a quality program. For example, emergency planning, first aid, and disaster response are all activities that must be part of a complete safety and health program, but are not necessarily a part of a quality program. Some companies set up an "element 4.21" for management system elements that do not come straight from the elements of the ISO and QS-9000 series.

Typical Noncompliances in a Safety Program Audit

- Safety and health manual is incomplete; outdated procedures are in the manual and actual operations are different.
- Hazard analysis is not performed as part of planning as specified in the procedure.

4.3 Contract Review

Establish and maintain documented procedures for contract review and coordination of these activities.

Guidelines for Safety Program Elements

In a quality management system, contract review is the process by which some of the explicit quality requirements of the customer are determined. These quality requirements form the basis for the entire quality system. Along with internal quality parameters and benchmarks from competitors, these define what quality means for the product or service, and what aspects of the process should be controlled and measured.

In a safety program, the "customer requirements" can be interpreted as the input that drives the safety program. This input includes:

- Laws and regulations that pertain to worker safety, such as OSHA standards
- Internal requirements, such as safety performance objectives or corporate guidelines
- Voluntary standards, such as industry sector standards or ANSI standards
- Labor union contract specifications relating to safety
- Insurance company recommendations
- Results of risk identification surveys by internal or third-party auditors

Your safety program should include provisions that describe your process for researching these requirements and ensuring that they are kept current. Assign accountability to a specific person for review and maintenance of a list of regulatory and other requirements for safety. Establish who will audit or survey operations to identify hazards in current and planned operations. The output of this process will enter into several other elements of your safety management system.

Guidelines for Safety Program Elements

Customer contracts and orders are the driving force that determines what and how products or services will be provided. Just as the quality system requires a system of review to be sure the supplier can meet the requirements, your safety program should include provisions to review contracts and orders for nonroutine process requirements that will require special safety procedures.

Include in your system an evaluation of orders with special requirements for products or services, covering:

- Customer specifications
- Process
- Unusual raw materials
- Packaging and shipping
- DOT labels
- Transportation
- Infield setup
- Testing

Just as the process engineering department may need to evaluate changes to production to meet the customer requirements, safety and health program considerations may need to be made to adjust to special orders.

A customer requirement for a special corrosion-resistant paint on a tank, for example, may be met by engineering with an order for a paint that contains a toxic pigment such as lead or chromium. While all other production requirements remain the same, the requirement for a toxic material adds a significant safety and health hazard to an otherwise routine operation. You may not be able to meet this customer requirement—not for process reasons, but for safety and health reasons.

Typical Noncompliances in a Safety Program Audit

- No copy of current OSHA standards at the facility, and no accountability for monitoring of regulatory requirements.
- Insurance company safety recommendations from study have not been addressed. No mechanism exists for review and disposition of recommendations.
- No baseline analysis of hazards has been performed.

4.4 Design Control

Control and verify the design of the product to ensure completeness in meeting specified customer requirements.

The safety function must be represented on R&D committees, engineering/marketing task forces, and in any function that produces new designs and processes. Ideally, a safety and health review will be included in all potential new product and service evaluations at the earliest concept stage. Along with questions on marketing, financial paybacks, and production engineering for new ideas, safety and health should be a prime consideration even at the R&D and pilot stages.

- Obtain all laws, regulations, and standards that apply to the operation or product.
- Competent staff should use Failure Mode and Effects Analysis, Fault Tree Analysis, or other appropriate techniques to anticipate and prevent hazards at the initial design stage.
- As production plans processes to make the product, it should include the establishment of human factors (ergonomic) requirements.
- Work instructions should be written to include safety procedures.
- Determine raw material toxicity, flammability, and reactivity hazards, and seek substitutes or alternative methods and materials that present less hazard.
- When past the initial concept stage, set safety and health requirements for pilot operations and R&D.
- Review the proposed manufacturing process for hazards (Job Safety Analysis).
- Design safety into the process. As an example, James M. Stone, Jr., former program manager for Morton Thiokol's airbag business, used four principles for reducing the potential number of explosions that occurred from the sodium azide raw material: Isolate all systems and operate them remotely; expect "incidents" and design for them, rather than trying to design a foolproof system; maintain twice the capacity required by forecasts; and "train, train, train."

- Establish and carry out the safety and health training needs of the manufacturing and servicing staff.
- Establish safety labeling requirements, advertising and catalog wording, user instructions, and service considerations.
- Determine safe waste-handling procedures and recycle/disposal requirements.

Typical Noncompliances in a Safety Program Audit

- Initial development and communication among marketing, R&D, and production design functions not recorded as called for in the procedure.
- No requirement exists for these functions to consider safety and health in their new product procedures.
- Workers use methyl ethyl ketone to clean up ink spills. No evaluation by engineering for a less hazardous cleaning procedure.
- Customer orders are reviewed by order-entry personnel, but there is no mechanism for including safety and health in the review process.
- Large quantity of flammables ordered (over capacity for proper storage without considering the special storage needs).

4.5 Document and Data Control

Control all documents and data related to quality.

Guidelines for Safety Program Elements

Documented procedures and records are the heart of the ISO 9000 quality standards. In this framework, they should be the heart of the safety and health program as well.

- Establish who has the authority to develop, approve, and maintain safety procedures and manual contents. This could include, for example, requiring the safety engineer's approval for all work instructions that include safety items.

- Specify the method to control safety manuals, procedures, and work instructions to ensure that all personnel have only the latest authorized edition and that current documents are available.
- Set up a system to ensure that obsolete documents are destroyed.
- Establish a control system to ensure that:
  - everyone that should have a document actually gets the current valid version;
  - all obsolete documents are destroyed and not used.
- Retain records and reports on the performance of the safety program and protect them in accordance with a set procedure. For example, OSHA requires that certain medical examinations of workers exposed to asbestos be kept for at least thirty years.
- Collect all relevant federal, state, and local regulations pertaining to safety and health, as well as all international, national, or industry standards. Maintain these in a database and assign responsibility for updates.

Typical Noncompliances in a Safety Program Audit

- Some workers in the stamping department have no access to safety procedures; the supervisor has outdated documents.
- Computerized database of procedures is backed up on floppies that are stored in the same desk that holds the PC with master files.
- Workers are using outdated safety procedure for tank entry.

4.6 Purchasing

Control purchased products and services, subcontractor, and suppliers to ensure that they meet specifications.

Guidelines for Safety Program Elements

Your system should be designed so that any raw materials, safety equipment, and services purchased are reviewed to ensure that they meet safety and health requirements just as they meet quality specifications.

- Establish safety and health requirements for purchased products, services, raw materials at the design stage (e.g., machine guards, ergonomics and human factors specifications, noise levels, toxicity, flammability, and requirements for special operating manuals, training, or lab certifications).
- Set purchasing requirement for material safety data sheets (MSDSs) to be sent with all chemicals. Ensure that the purchasing process specifies that these requirements are part of the ordering system.
- Include safety requirements in the system for review and testing or inspection of incoming materials and equipment.
- Establish lists of approved vendors of safety supplies and equipment (e.g., use only labs that have requisite certifications and safety equipment that meets standards). Just as you would not continue to buy from vendors who do not meet quality requirements, restrict purchases from contractors who do not meet safety requirements.
- Include the procedures for dealing with outside contractors in your program. There are two considerations in this element: The contractor's employees should be protected from hazards they are exposed to from your

operations, just like your own staff, and you need to be assured that the contractor does not introduce new hazards to your environment as well.

- Make provisions in your program to select, train, and control safety performance of subcontractors working in the plant, performing service on product, or working at customer sites.
- Insert safety requirements into the purchase order or contracting procedure, and require an orientation and training session with contractor employees that mirrors the training done for your own staff.

For example, many companies require that all visitors to their site view an orientation video, review written safety procedures, sign a form acknowledging their understanding before they are allowed on the premises, and follow safety rules and use appropriate personal protective equipment while in the facility.

Typical Noncompliances in a Safety Program Audit

- No MSDSs were found for the chemicals received.
- The system does not require any safety specifications in the purchasing process.
- Contractors work in the plant with no training or introduction to the safety and health procedures required.
- Contractor workers installing carpeting using flammable adhesives without the knowledge of the plant staff.
- The auditor conducting an industrial hygiene evaluation of the rocket propellant plant is told by an employee: "If you hear a 'boom!,' look and see what everyone else is doing. If they start to run, follow them." This is the total extent of safety and health training for visitors.

4.7 Control of Customer-Supplied Product

Control verification, storage, and maintenance of products supplied by customers.

Guidelines for Safety Program Elements

In the context of a quality system, materials that are supplied by the customer might be assumed to automatically meet specifications. Special provision is made in the ISO standards to avoid this assumption and to ensure that customer-supplied product is appropriately treated.

In the context of safety and health, the same requirements for any purchased materials of equipment apply to those received from customers. You should apply the same procedures for setting standards for incoming materials: inspect them, test them, store them properly, and maintain them for suitability for production.

Typical Noncompliances in a Safety Program Audit

- Customer-supplied materials are not included in the safety specification system for receiving inspection; an explosive material found in the receiving area without an accompanying MSDS.

4.8 Product Identification and Traceability

Establish and maintain a system for tracing the product at all stages from receipt of raw material to installation, servicing, and disposal.

Guidelines for Safety Program Elements

Product quality requires that raw materials be traced through the process so that noncompliances can be identified and corrected at their root-cause level. Similarly, a raw material should be labeled and traceable for safety and health reasons. At any stage in the production process, employees (and customers) should be able to learn, through labeling and easily found documentation, the hazards of the materials they work with.

- Establish a chemical inventory system for all raw materials used in the organization. Include in the system a method for updating the list and reviewing additions for safety and health information.
- Provide for the collection and storage of MSDSs that are available to all employees who use the materials.
- Provide for retention of original DOT, NFPA, UN, or other hazard and identification labels for all incoming materials and equipment.
- Develop a method for maintaining the traceability of the material's characteristics through the production process. The process will also be useful in the event of a defective product that may pose a hazard to workers or customers (e.g., a contaminated batch of a raw material can be traced to find the shipped product lots that may pose a hazard). For example, current OSHA standards require that chemicals remain with their original safety labels and that the working containers they are transferred in be labeled with the potential hazards associated with the chemical.
- Label material transportation systems such as pipes and material conveyors as well as containers.

Typical Noncompliances in a Safety Program Audit

- No chemical inventory.
- Unlabeled chemical containers found in the plant; no system established for requiring labels on containers of chemicals after they are transferred to working containers.

4.9 Process Control

Identify and plan the manufacturing process to assure that it is carried out under controlled conditions.

Guidelines for Safety Program Elements

When work procedures are developed for quality reasons, they should also be developed for safety considerations. Your program should include the appropriate engineering, administrative, or personal protective equipment controls for each process, based on the safety and health hazards identified in the design or baseline identification process. In the ISO context, "suitable" work environment and equipment should include "safe" as well as suitable for quality.

- Apply the risk management protocol for control of hazards:
  - — Avoid the hazard by eliminating the operation or material that presents it: Do it another way. Example: Use a flux-free soldering process to avoid the use of cleaning materials.
  - — Substitute a less toxic or hazardous material that will still do the job. Example: Use a water-based cleaner instead of an organic solvent.
  - — Control the hazard with engineering controls designed to prevent the hazardous condition from causing an accident; design the control in a fail-safe mode. Example: Use a ventilation system with interlocks that shut down the operation or sound an alarm if airflow fails, and guards that shut off power to equipment if removed.
  - — Use personal protective equipment (PPE). Example: If all other techniques still leave a potential hazard, provide gloves, respirators, and clothing. Note that PPE is the least preferred method of protection, because it is a last barrier to the hazard, and relies on

workers' behavior to be effective—employees must understand its proper use and follow procedures at all times for PPE to be effective.

- Determine which process parameters need to be monitored and controlled for safety. If a chemical reaction is part of the process, should there be monitoring of temperature and pressure? What are the parameters that affect safety?
- Include maintenance of safety control equipment such as guards, ventilation, temperature and pressure monitoring, and electrical fault detection and protection, as well as process control equipment.
- Establish procedures to ensure that all current and potential hazards are controlled in a timely manner through engineering techniques if possible: those that do not rely on workers following a procedure. There should be mechanisms in place that assure that safe work practices are understood and followed by all workers.

IBM's ECAT Division safety staff took advantage of its company's ISO 9000 effort to include safety in the writing of work procedures. Its safety director noted cases where workers were lifting boxes over 25 pounds; as part of the process redesign, it added handles to the boxes to prevent back strains. Workers using alcohol to clean parts developed skin rashes; the use of gloves was written into the work procedure and the rashes went away. Workstations were redesigned to eliminate awkward reaching, and muscle strains and sprains diminished while productivity increased.

Typical Noncompliances in a Safety Program Audit

- Ventilation systems are in place, but are poorly designed so that contaminants can be seen escaping.
- No machine guards on power presses.
- Employees found wearing respirators with only one strap.

- Workers bend over to lift heavy cases up onto a conveyor line.
- No upper temperature specification for a degreaser.

4.10 Inspection and Testing

Establish and carry out procedures for testing to ensure that the product meets quality specifications.

Guidelines for Safety Program Elements

Provide for routine testing of safety and health hazards and controls. Include documentation and preservation of records and a system of corrective actions for failures and noncompliances. Some examples include:

- Safety and health inspections of the workplace to find hazards.
- Measurement of hazards that are not easily detected by normal inspection or observation, such as industrial hygiene exposures like noise, dust and fume levels, and radiation.
- The testing of engineering control and protective equipment through inspection of safety equipment such as eyewash fountains, showers, fire extinguishers, fire-detection devices, machine guards, ventilation systems, robotic controls, interlocks, respirators, etc.
- Include inspection of mechanical devices such as hoists and chains.

Typical Noncompliances in a Safety Program Audit

- No records of periodic measurement of noise or other industrial hygiene exposures.
- Incoming materials and equipment are not checked for matching of safety requirements.
- Fire extinguishers found with expired indicators and status.
- Workers using respirators with expired cartridges.

4.11 Control of Inspection, Measuring, and Test Equipment

Establish and maintain procedures to control, calibrate, and maintain test and measurement equipment.

Guidelines for Safety Program Elements

The most frequent testing of exposures will result in a false sense of security if the equipment used is not calibrated and the test results are wrong.

- Establish and maintain calibration programs for measuring equipment. Examples include industrial hygiene air sampling devices, electrical test devices, and velometers for ventilation system monitoring.
- If samples of air, water, biological material, or chemicals are sent to a laboratory for analysis, the lab should have a quality control program and appropriate accreditation. You may wish to establish a program of sending spiked or blind samples to the lab to test its reliability.

Typical Noncompliances in a Safety Program Audit

- No calibration labels or records of calibration for an air flow measurement instrument.
- Air samples to monitor workers' exposures to lead are sent to a nonaccredited, unqualified lab.

4.12 Inspection and Test Status

Identify the inspection and test status of all product pertaining to conformance or nonconformance.

Guidelines for Safety Program Elements

After testing of safety equipment is done, there must be a system that yields ready verification of its proper functioning.

- Tag all safety equipment such as showers, eyewash fountains, ventilation systems, and guards with an identification of the current calibration and test status. The tag should contain the date of last test, the status, and the initials of the person doing the test.
- Similarly, tag or label any test equipment used for the above to show its calibration status.
- Color code equipment so that hazardous conditions are flagged; for example, Ford uses alert orange to color the parts of machines that are covered by guards, so when the guard is removed, the orange shows and alerts the operator to the hazard.
- Establish a documentation system that shows the current test status of all critical safety equipment and controls the frequency of testing and calibration.

Typical Noncompliances in a Safety Program Audit

- Nonfunctioning eyewash fountains found with no indication of having been inspected.

4.13 Control of Nonconforming Product

Systems should be in place to ensure that all product that does not conform to specifications is not used or installed.

Guidelines for Safety Program Elements

- Establish a system to prevent equipment from being used if it has not passed inspection or been tested for safety requirements (e.g., test equipment that is out of calibration, damaged guards on machinery).

This will rely on proper training of all personnel so that they understand that equipment that is not identified as being tested and acceptable should be assumed to be out of control, and not to be used.

Typical Noncompliances in a Safety Program Audit

- Machinery operating without proper guards in place.
- Fire extinguishers that indicate low charge but are still in use.
- Airflow measuring equipment in use with no calibration tag.

4.14 Corrective and Preventive Action

Take and document actions to correct or prevent product nonconformities on the basis of customer complaints and other sources of information.

Guidelines for Safety Program Elements

There are many sources of information about nonconformancies in the safety and health system: Your program should have procedures for examination and analysis of loss reports from insurance carriers, accident investigations, "near-miss" incident reports, internal and consultant audits, and OSHA inspections. Employee reports of safety hazards or noncompliance with the program should be treated as customer complaints, because employees are the recipients of the service provided by the safety and health program. The analysis of this data, particularly accident investigations, should include a mechanism for establishing the "root cause" of the incident.

- Establish regular management review of formal corrective action reports, the analysis of those reports, and corrective action recommendations. For example, a compilation of the recommendations for safety and health program improvements submitted by internal auditors, consultants, safety committees or teams, OSHA, or insurance company inspectors should be reviewed by management and action taken to implement the recommendations.
- Keep and control records of corrective actions taken as a result of these reviews. Subsequent internal audits of the program should review these records and report on the actions taken.

- Set up a system for employee reporting of hazardous conditions. Provision should be made so that there is no penalty for reporting, and employees are not discouraged from making timely and frank reports.

Typical Noncompliances in a Safety Program Audit

- Management review meeting minutes show that eye injuries continue to occur. Several meetings have noted this with no action taken for prevention.
- Employees report machine guards removed by maintenance and not replaced. No management inquiry made to maintenance to correct operation.

4.15 Handling, Storage, Packaging, Preservation, and Delivery

Establish and maintain procedures to ensure the preservation of quality product after manufacture.

Guidelines for Safety Program Elements

After a product is made, employees must handle, store, package, and deliver the product. This introduces transportation and material handling hazards. Whereas this quality requirement is another ISO 9000 element that has no direct parallel in a safety and health program, the activities that an organization conducts in this area present a set of potential safety and health problems that need to be addressed.

- Identify material handling hazards and include prevention methods in your program.
- Set procedures for evaluation and development of ergonomically correct handling of materials.
- Set requirements for warehousing and storage facilities: for example, rack heights, ventilation, fire protection, grounding and bonding, and accessibility.

- Implement a forklift-driver safety program in accordance with OSHA standards.
- Establish machine guarding requirements for labeling and packaging equipment.
- Provide proper equipment and procedures for delivery personnel, including ergonomic assessments of the process and training for the workers.
- If your employees actually deliver product, a complete fleet safety program may be needed. Vehicles need to be selected with safety in mind, and routine maintenance and inspection programs developed. Provide training, such as DOT driver training programs for truck drivers.

Typical Noncompliances in a Safety Program Audit

- Delivery personnel carrying excessive loads on handcarts to meet delivery schedules; back injuries found to be a leading source of lost-time injuries.
- Delivery trucks found with broken side-view mirrors.
- Forklift driver observed dropping a skid of parts while taking a corner at high speed.

4.16 Control of Quality Records

Procedures for identification, collection, storage, indexing, access, maintenance, and disposition of records.

Guidelines for safety program elements

- Define what safety and health program documents are considered important enough to control and retain. These may include such records as accident investigations, OSHA reports, inspection and test status of safety equipment, corrective action reports, and audit results. The program manual and any safety and health procedures should be included.

- Consult with your legal department to identify those records that are required to be controlled or retained by statute.
- Establish written procedures for the collection and retention of these safety documents.
- Minutes of management review meetings regarding safety and health should be kept for future review when assessing the effectiveness of the system.
- Establish a control system to ensure that:
  - — records are retained for the proper period. (Define retention periods for records, based on corporate policy and regulatory requirements. Records should not be kept longer than specified, nor should they be destroyed prematurely. If a case goes to court and you destroyed records prematurely, you may be suspected or accused of a "coverup.");
  - — computer records are secure and backed up on a scheduled basis.

Typical Noncompliances in a Safety Program Audit

- Computer database backup tapes kept in the same desk with the PC hard drive containing originals.
- Safety committee meeting minutes for the last two years missing from the file; procedure calls for five-year retention.
- No system exists describing what records to store, where to store them, or how long to store records.
- No records are kept of inspections by safety consultants or insurance company inspectors.

4.17 Internal Quality Audits

Set up a system of conducting audits of quality procedures and recommending and recording corrective actions.

Guidelines for Safety Program Elements

- To ensure that the safety program itself is carried out as designed, conduct periodic regular audits of the safety program activities. This should be done by staff other than those responsible for the safety program. It is important to remember that this audit is *not* a safety inspection; it is an audit of the *program*. The audit should be done in essentially the same manner as an ISO 9000 internal audit of the quality program: Objective evidence in the form of documentation should be collected to establish that each element of the safety and health program is indeed being done as written. At one major corporation, independent audits of the internal auditing system are conducted to assure that the audit system itself is performing.

One of the most important elements of a good safety and health program is the initial and ongoing program to identify all potential hazards in the workplace. This function is not directly addressed in the ISO 9000 series, although ISO 14001 does call for an initial evaluation of an organization's environmental impacts. (See also element 4.3, Contract Review, page 48.)

- Conduct baseline and periodic comprehensive worksite surveys for safety and health.
- Make up the audit team with competent persons who have training in safety and health appropriate to the level of hazards that may be expected in the workplace. For example, a chemical plant may require industrial hygiene specialists and chemical engineers on the audit team, whereas an office facility may need a survey team with less demanding technical credentials.

- The surveyors must be accompanied by the staff who have responsibility for operations on a daily basis. This not only ensures that accurate information is transmitted to specialists, but assures that the workers who will be there permanently will have the benefit of hands-on experience in identification of hazards.
- Include analysis of planned and new facilities, processes, materials, and equipment as well as routine job hazards.
- Investigate accidents and "near-miss" incidents to identify their causes and means for prevention.
- Cover operations that occur only infrequently or at times or places that are easily forgotten: night shifts, maintenance of storage tanks, operations at remote sites.
- Schedule regular and frequent periodic site safety and health inspections, so that new operations or previously missed hazards and failures in hazard controls are identified.
- Establish a system to encourage employees, without fear of reprisal, to notify management personnel about conditions that appear hazardous. The system should include a procedure that requires timely and appropriate responses, to further encourage employees to report on hazards.
- The internal audit reports and recommendations for corrective actions should be reviewed by top management, and a record kept of corrective actions taken.

Typical Noncompliances in a Safety Program Audit

- Audit by an insurance carrier discovers hazards not noted by plant safety staff. No independent staff had audited the program to ascertain if a thorough baseline had been performed.
- Activities of local plant safety coordinator is done on a "put out fires" basis. There is no program to determine priorities based on degree of risk.

- Accident investigation file does not contain reports on several accidents listed in Workers' Compensation report files.
- Workers point out several hazards to auditor and state that they never reported them to management because "nothing ever gets done about them, anyway."

4.18 Training

Identify, carry out, and record all training needs of personnel.

Guidelines for Safety Program Elements

Training is one of the most important components of a quality or a safety and health program. Workers must be shown how to perform a procedure and why it is important if the end result is to be reached. All safety program elements have some degree of training inherent in them. Some that have specific regulatory requirements for training include hazard communication (right to know), forklift-driver training, lock and tag out, hazardous waste operations (Hazwoper), confined space entry, and respirator use. In addition, OSHA has specific regulations for working with many chemical agents, such as asbestos and lead, that require training of workers.

Your safety and health training program has several objectives. These include:

- Teaching employees (both your own and those of contractors) the specific safety procedures that are part of their routine job.
- Ensuring that all employees understand the hazards to which they may be exposed and how to prevent harm to themselves and others.
- Ensuring that supervisors and managers understand their safety responsibilities and the management system they operate within.

The program should:

- Determine what training is required, both by regulation and for the purpose of reducing hazards and the probability of accidents.
- Find out who needs training.
- Assure that everyone is trained.
- Measure the effectiveness of the training.
- Keep records of who was trained when.
- Schedule employees for retraining at routine intervals and after job changes.
- Ensure that those doing the training are themselves qualified to do so.

Typical Noncompliances in a Safety Program Audit

- Employee is unable to answer when asked if he or she understands the hazards of the chemical in a drum at the work site.
- Employees are found cleaning up a spill in the production area and misusing respirators because they had never been trained in proper use.
- Contractor employees are unaware of plant nonsmoking restrictions.

4.19 Servicing

Establish and maintain documented procedures for ensuring that servicing is carried out in compliance with specifications.

Guidelines for Safety Program Elements

Servicing of product is one of those easily forgotten operations, especially if it is carried out on the premises of the customer. If there is a service operation in your organization, it should be included in all parts of your safety and health program. In a sense, your service personnel are the equivalent of outside contractors working in your plant: They must be aware of the safety and health considerations of their own jobs as well as those that may be encountered at the customer's site, or en route to it.

- Evaluate off-site operations for hazards and establish safety procedures for off-site work by staff.
- Provide driver safety training for delivery and sales personnel.
- Label your vehicles with a "1-800" number for reporting of vehicle or driver problems.
- Train service personnel in the hazards of the operations they may carry out at a customer's location, and require them to inform customer staff of the potential hazards; likewise, service personnel must inquire of the customer if there are any safety and health procedures that are to be followed by visitors.

Typical Noncompliances in a Safety Program Audit

- Service driver involved in an accident is found to be driving on a suspended license; no program to check motor vehicle records for tickets or suspensions.
- No driver training program for service personnel.

4.20 Statistical Techniques

Identify and use appropriate statistical measurement techniques for assuring quality of product.

Guidelines for Safety Program Elements

Just as you measure the incidence and statistical distribution of noncompliance in products, the actual results of the safety and health program must be measured.

- Establish statistical loss and incident analysis procedures to measure the performance of the safety program. Compare the results to the program objectives. Include data from sources like:
  - — Insurance loss reports (number and dollar amounts of claims, sorted by location, shift, type of injury, body part, operation, etc.).
  - — First aid and injury logs. For example, in trying to establish the cause of a rash of dermatitis cases for contractor employees working in a pharmaceutical plant, the first aid log gave the location of the project each worker was assigned to. A list of the cases sorted by location pinpointed the source as a new antibiotic pilot plant, resulting in protective measures for workers in that area.
  - — Incident reports (number of incidents, sorted by location, operation, etc.).
  - — OSHA or state inspections (lists of violations).
  - — Insurance company inspections (recommendations for correction of hazards).
  - — Consultant services reports.
  - — Air sampling data (measurement of industrial hygiene exposures).
- Analyze injury and illness trends over extended periods so that patterns with common causes can be identified and prevented.
- Benchmark against your industry group and competitors to determine objectives and performance criteria to measure your progress.
- Do Pareto analysis of accident and near-miss statistics to help establish priorities for action and direct attention to the most frequent and severe problems. (A Pareto analysis is a listing of data in descending order of frequency, so that the categories with the most impact on the total are listed first. By concentrating on the 20 percent of

accident causes that result in 80 percent of the incidents; for example, you can determine four or five categories that need priority action. Corrective action in these few categories can result in eliminating most of the injuries or accidents.)

- If your organization has so few accidents that a statistical analysis does not reveal any useful information, use industrywide statistics to highlight hazards that you should control. Or you can keep records of near misses: incidents that do not result in injury or property damage, but clearly had the potential to do so.

Typical Noncompliances in a Safety Program Audit

- Insurance inspector points out to the personnel manager at a financial service company that a loss report is available for injuries reported to the insurance carrier. The intent is to help the manager find the largest sources of Workers' Compensation injuries for his office. The manager's response is, "What do I do with that?" Personnel manager should have known the purpose of review of losses.
- Plant manager mandates safety-shoe and hard hat program in a plant even though a Workers' Compensation report indicates 50 percent of lost time results from sprains and strains due to material handling. No corrective action records are found related to sprains and strains of the work force.

III

CHAPTER 5

ISO 9000 AND YOUR PRODUCT SAFETY PROGRAM

As explained in previous chapters, product safety is an essential element of product quality. But we have found from experience that product safety is sometimes overlooked even in companies that have developed an ISO or QS-9000 program and measured its results. Because product quality is already embedded in the ISO/QS-9000 requirements, we do not need to fit them into the ISO framework—they *are* the framework. This chapter is formatted to highlight the ISO/QS-9000 requirements for product safety that exist in the standards.

We have added examples of typical noncompliances found in ISO and QS audits. These are based on the author's experience in manufacturing and as an auditor of both ISO 9000 and QS-9000 systems. This chapter uses examples from the 1995 CPSC "Safety Sells" Conference. Sanitized product recalls are also provided to illustrate prevention strategies. These and the examples of noncompliances have been sanitized for confidentiality.

4.1 Management Responsibility

Define and document policy for quality, including objectives for quality and commitment to quality.

Guidelines for Product Safety Programs

Commitment by executive management to the quality policy and its objectives is essential. Executive management is ultimately responsible for effective operations, which includes producing safe and reliable products and services. Key resource and financial decisions made by executive management affect the entire organization. Without top-level support, the ISO 9000 effort, including the product safety component, will not be successful.

4.1.1 Quality Policy

Guidelines for Product Safety Programs

- Include statements within the policy regarding safety and reliability of products and/or services and a commitment to continuous improvement and to customer satisfaction.
- Define safety objectives clearly so that all employees are informed, understand, and are committed to the policy. State them so that employees know how their job relates to the quality objectives.
- Have the top executive sign the policy and quality manual, and communicate the policy to the entire workforce.
- Increase visibility of the policy. Place it in the lobby, lunchroom, newsletters, advertising, etc.

Example: Procter & Gamble's human and product safety policy is very straightforward: "It is our policy that our products shall be safe for humans and the environment, either used as intended or under conditions of reasonably foreseeable accidental misuse. We want safety during the manufacturing, warehousing, presentation for sale, consumer storage, and ultimately, when products and packages find their way into the environment, either totally or in part."

4.1.2 Organization

Guidelines for Product Safety Programs

This clause requires the establishment of the lines of responsibility, authority, interrelations, and dedication of resources for an effective system.

- Establish a cross-functional quality steering committee. Include within this steering committee top management, and key people responsible for product and workplace safety. Each member should be at the executive level. An example is Whirlpool Corporation's quality and safety committees. They are chaired by their vice president for manufacturing and technology, North American Appliance Group.
- Develop organizational charts showing reporting structures and verification personnel. Indicate clearly all departments, including centralized functions and their interrelations. Show interrelations of corporate functions to division and plant levels. Examples of functions to include are:
    - Centralized design
    - Administration
    - Executive management
    - Maintenance
    - Quality
    - Environmental
    - Production
    - Accounting
    - Service
    - Shipping/receiving
    - Reliability and R&D labs
    - Legal
    - Purchasing
    - Safety and health
    - Regulatory compliance
    - Information systems
    - Sales and marketing
    - Repair
- Illustrate "organizational freedom"—the independence necessary for effective operation—for the verification

personnel. They should have "stop work" authority. An example of a situation of lack of organizational freedom that affected product safety:

— A quality manager reports to the plant manager in an OEM plastics plant. The product is safety-related and must meet Federal Motor Vehicle Safety Standards (FMVSS). The plant also ships to customers using "just-in-time" inventory and delivery methods. The inspection department finds failures during random testing, which are promptly reported to the quality manager, who puts a hold on the product. The lab immediately rechecks calibration of the test device, retests the samples, and confirms the failure. Further samples are tested: Results show a 25 percent failure rate. The situation calls for 100 percent test, which is called for by the quality manager. The time delay necessitates premium freight to make the shipment deadline. The plant manager overrules the quality manager, and nonconforming product is knowingly shipped as directed. The customer is not notified. This would be considered a major noncompliance in any ISO or QS-9000 audit. In this case, it is also against the law to knowingly ship defective safety-related products (under the National Highway Transportation Safety Act).

Conflicts of interest like this arise often; this is why establishing organizational freedom is an extremely important point in developing an ISO or QS-9000 program.

4.1.2.2 Resources

Guidelines for Product Safety Programs

This clause requires your company to provide adequate resources to produce safe and reliable products, including competent people and capable equipment. The keywords "qualified" and "trained" are an important distinction to add to each of these resources.

A major potential pitfall in many programs may be lack of funding for proper resource allocation in R&D, inadequate development and safety testing, and incapable equipment, which very likely could result in product failures, recalls, and potential injury to consumers. Product safety recalls and design defects are not acceptable, and must be prevented before they occur. Omissions and oversight in this critical stage of product development simply cannot be tolerated, and must be communicated to all responsible parties.

- Identify minimum qualifications for all verification personnel. Include education, experience, license, certification, and training.
- Describe where these qualifications are found: in job descriptions, classification handbooks, databases, etc.
- Establish methods to measure staff utilization and staffing needs. For example, Procter & Gamble utilizes a ratio of one R&D staff having responsibility for the safety of its products and packages for every eight of its R&D staff worldwide.
- Provide feedback or performance reviews to all verification personnel.
- Establish methods such as project planning, costing, capacity planning, forecasting, to determine equipment requirements.
- Include state-of-the-art design, development, processing, and testing equipment as required to stay current with evolving consumer safety needs.

4.1.3 Management Review

Guidelines for Product Safety Programs

ISO and QS-9000 require that the supplier's management with executive responsibility shall review the quality system at defined intervals. The review must be sufficient to ensure the system's continuing suitability and effectiveness in meeting the requirements of this standard as well as the supplier's stated quality policy and objectives (see 4.1.1). Records of such reviews shall be maintained (see 4.16).

Figure 5.1 illustrates management review from a macro perspective. To back up the performance indicators, further detail would typically be attached. (For example, Ford suppliers are required to establish and use performance indicators as described in the *Ford Operating System Manual.*)

- As part of the review process, specify measurables and goals. Measure items like customer complaints, audit results and actions, accident reports, and product safety issues stemming from any customer complaints. Management then should assign resources for continued improvement and monitor the status of corrective actions until closure.
- Set a regular schedule for an entire system audit. Audit all departments. Include all safety-related procedures.
- Set up frequent (monthly or better) management reviews of items related to product safety.
- Assign resources and completion dates for safety action items.
- Report progress on open issues and corrective actions.
- Keep minutes of the meeting for the record.
- Focus on prevention and corrective actions for product safety problems.
- Determine priorities based on any safety-related issues, including recall plans.

Figure 5.1
Management Review Web Chart

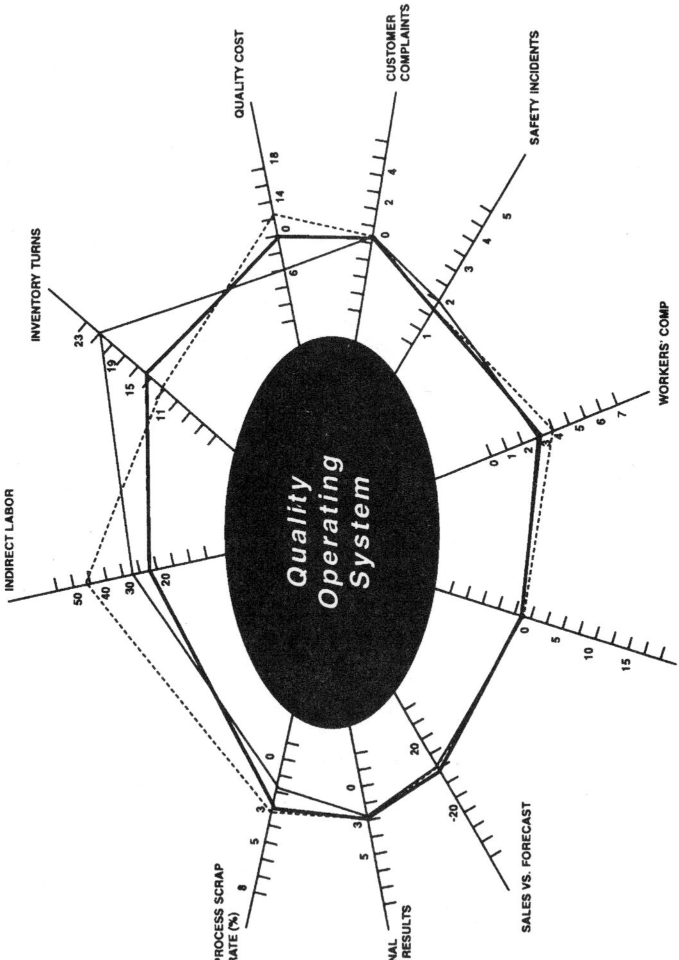

4.1.4 (QS-9000) Business Plan

Guidelines for Product Safety Programs

The supplier shall formalize a formal, documented, comprehensive business plan. This plan may typically include as applicable:... health, safety, and environmental issues.... Methods to track, update, revise, and review the plan shall be communicated throughout the organization as appropriate.

Strategic planning is typically driven by sales, marketing, and executive management. What is a requirement for a business plan doing in a quality standard? Quality, safety and health, and the environment are becoming more significant in business planning. Designing safety into products, systems, and worker safety and health can be a part of a profitable strategy for your company. Look at what's happening in the automobile industry:

- The Insurance Institute for Highway Safety reports that Ford's completely redesigned 1996 Taurus leads the way in the Institute's crash worthiness evaluation program. It tops 14 other popular four-door midsize cars. The only identified weakness was the poor design of the head restraints. Ford advertises that "Only your mother is more obsessed with your safety." Driver safeguards described in the ad include a traction control system, antilock brakes, dual airbags, 24-hour roadside assistance, and the vision enhancement system now under development.
- Major auto suppliers are partnering with auto manufacturers to develop new safety and health technologies. As reported in *Popular Mechanics*, Delphi Chassis Systems is developing the Traxxar stability control system for General Motors. Other suppliers such as Bosch and ITT are working on similar systems.
- *Inc. Magazine* described Allen Breed as its Entrepreneur of the Year in December 1995. Breed first pitched Chrysler in 1967 on his idea: Equip every car with airbags. His airbag manufacturing company passed $324 million in sales in

1994. Breed is now one of the most profitable auto industry suppliers, and lives are being saved by his product.

Include safety and health in your business plan, as well as evaluations of safety and health and environmental regulations and your competitor's and supplier's new technology in these areas.

Typical Noncompliances in Quality Systems Audit

- In a 1995 audit, a business plan is found dated June 1992.
- Management review minutes are found with no measure of customer complaints. Also, the past two of three management review meeting records are not found.
- Management review records are found without specific goals for safety-related parameters as required by procedure.
- Management review records found from the last quarter with no mention of follow-up status to action items from last meetings. Further investigation shows open customer complaints dating back six months.

4.2 Quality System

Establish, maintain, and document the overall management system for quality, including procedures and work instructions.

Guidelines for Product Safety Programs

This element covers a structured approach for establishing and maintaining a quality manual and procedures covering all elements of the relevant standards. The intent is to provide an easily understood framework of documentation for employees to use. Without this written framework, workers may not understand how the system works, what their responsibility is in the system, and what the overall objective of the program is. If that happens, product safety, as well as the overall quality of the service or product, will not meet customer expectations. This documentation should be used as a training tool.

The standard places emphasis on prevention and actions to correct failures. Each procedure should have a contingency for what to do to prevent a failure, and what to do in the event of failure. You should determine failure modes relative to product safety for each functional area in your organization. Ask yourself the questions, "What do I do if it doesn't work the way it's supposed to?" and "How do I fix it?" For example, the shipping department could damage a drum, causing a chemical spill. Your plan should have a mechanism to foresee these types of failures and specify corrective actions to take if they occur.

4.2.2 Quality System Procedures

Guidelines for Product Safety Programs

Each department in an organization has at least some quality procedures. The following quality system procedures typically involve product safety:

- Management reviews
- Feasibility review
- Advance quality planning
- Failure mode effects analysis/control plans
- Contract review
- Design and development
- Drawing and specification control
- Engineering change control
- Purchasing
- Product traceability and identification
- Inspection and testing
- Equipment calibration
- Nonconforming product and material
- Production scheduling
- Supplier development
- PPAP production approval
- Benchmarking and satisfaction
- Preventive maintenance
- Environmental controls
- Training evaluation
- Hiring and training
- Shipping and delivery
- Process capability
- Receiving inspection
- Inventory and preservation
- Electronic data control
- Packaging and labeling
- Servicing and repair
- Reliability testing

Preventive and corrective action

Customer complaint

Statistical process control

Quality records

Internal audits

Documenting and formatting policy, procedure, and work instruction

Tooling fabrication and maintenance

Continuous improvement

MIS data and disaster recovery

For your procedures to be effective in preventing product safety problems, consider the following tips:

- Include details and clear acceptance criteria relevant to product safety.
- Limit procedures in length, and keep the steps in sequential order.
- Establish ownership by charging department heads and workers with documenting their own procedure(s).
- Collaborate with successfully registered firms and get samples/models of their procedures.
- Highlight your copy of the ISO/QS-9000 standard in color. Identify all "shalls, shoulds, and musts," along with keywords such as "records" and "safety" to help visualize and focus on requirements of ISO/QS-9000.
- Specify what data to record, who will record them, and how, when, and where to record them.
- Use photos or representative samples and date/approve for acceptance criteria where words don't easily or clearly describe the desired quality criteria for the work.
- Establish failure modes for each departmental procedure and build in prevention steps.
- Provide review and feedback on all procedures by a steering committee.

4.2.3 Quality Planning

Guidelines for Product Safety Programs

This clause is a high-ranking activity for product liability prevention. Quality planning is product- or process-specific and must occur prior to, and during, production. Customer requirements based on drawings, specifications, and purchase order requirements drive quality plans. This section also calls for updating quality plans as engineering changes and/or customer feedback may require.

For example, Pillsbury, NASA, and Natrick Labs developed a technique called Hazard Analysis Critical Control Point (HACCP). HACCP is a tool to identify and prevent food hazards in the food processing industry, rather than simply to detect them after production. The technique analyzes the flow of food through the process, monitors the process frequently, and defines the points that are critical for the control of food-borne disease hazards. Although not yet law, HACCP has become a valuable voluntary program for process control of microbial hazards, and is being adopted by progressive food companies.

Many automotive suppliers fail to identify the safety characteristic on the control plan. Also suppliers sometimes fail to revise control plans when required, such as incapable process (<1.33 CpK), when processes are changed, when product has changed, or when the process becomes unstable. Figure 5.2 illustrates the steps and linkages of quality planning tools.

Note that QS-9000 requires that safety and special characteristics must be carried out onto these working documents so that people are aware of their significance. QS-9000 also requires cross-functional teams for quality planning. Figure 5.3 illustrates a typical control plan as found in the Advance Production Quality Planning manual in QS-9000.

Figure 5.2
Quality Planning Diagram Based on AIAG's Advanced Product Quality Planning Manual

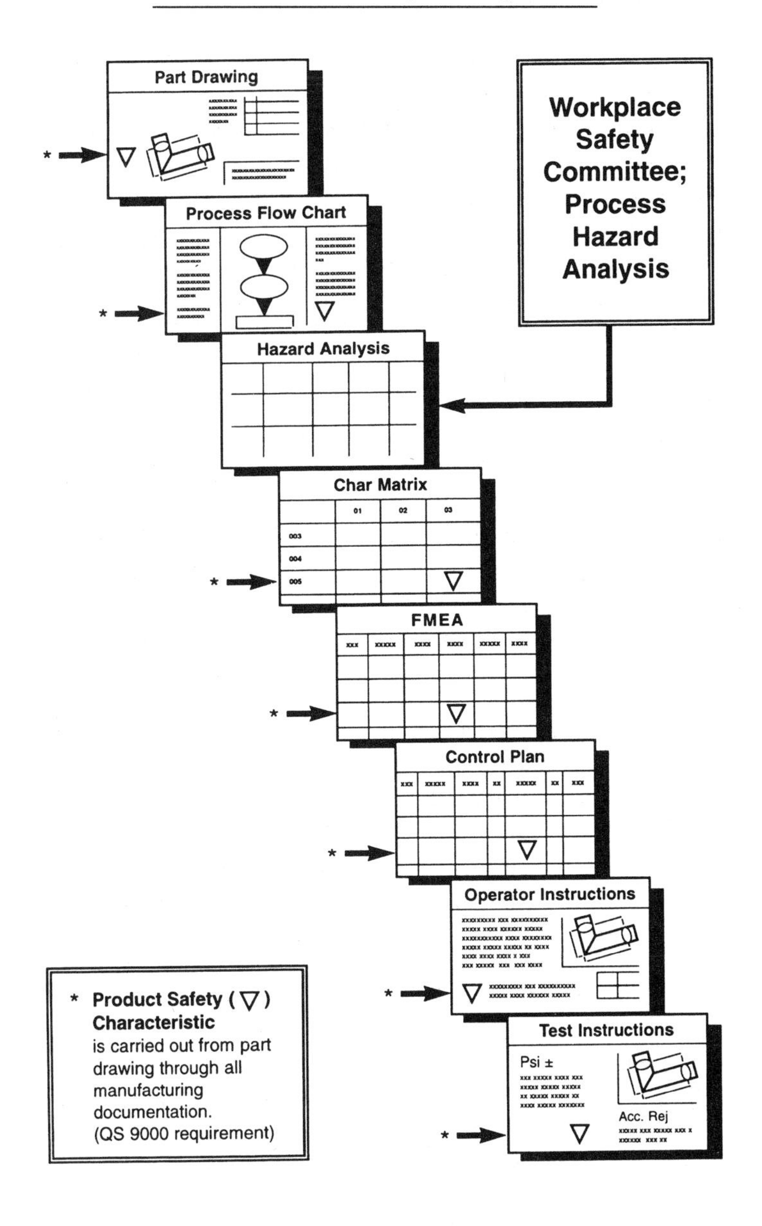

Figure 5.3: Control Plan

[ ] Prototype [ ] Pre-launch [X] Production Control Plan Number 001	Key Contact/Phone J. Davis / 313-555-5555	Date (Orig.) 1-26-92	Date (Rev.) 2-2-92
Part Number/Latest Change Level 22521211/G 11-2-92	Core Team Product Development Team (E01) - See list	Customer Engineering Approval/Date (If Req'd)	
Part Name/Description Plastic Injection Molded Grill	Supplier/Plant Approval/Date	Customer Quality Approval Date (If Req'd)	
Supplier/Plant 4-B Grill C. Plant #3 / Supplier Code	Other Approval/Date (If Req'd)	Other Approval/Date (If Req'd)	

Part/ Process Number	Process Name/ Operation Description	Machine, Device, Jig, Tools For Mfg.	Characteristics			Special Char. Class	Methods					Reaction Plan
			No.	Product	Process		Product/Process Specification/ Tolerance	Evaluation Measurement Technique	Prototype Size	Prototype Freq.	Control Method	
3	Plastic Injection Molding	Machine No. 1-5	18	Appearance		•	Free of blemishes	Visual inspection	100%	Continuous	100% Inspection	Notify Supervisor
				No blemishes			flowlines	1st piece buy-off			Check sheet	Adjust/recheck
							sink marks	1st piece buy-off			Check sheet	Adjust/recheck
		Machine No. 1-5	19	Mounting hole loc.		•	Hole "X" location	Fixture #10	1st piece	buy-off per run	Check sheet	Adjust/recheck
							25 +/- 1mm		5 pcs	hr	$\bar{X}$-R chart	Quarantine and adjust
		Machine No. 1-5	20	Dimension		•	Gap 3 +/- .5mm	Fixture #10	1st piece	buy-off per run	Check sheet	Adjust and recheck
		Fixture #10	21	Perimeter fit		•	Gap 3 +/- .5mm	Check gap to fixture 4 locations	5 pcs	hr	$\bar{X}$-R chart	Quarantine and adjust
		Machine No. 1-5	22		Set-up of mold machine		See attached set-up card	Review of set-up card and machine settings		Each set-up	1st piece buy-off	Adjust and reset machine
											Inspector verifies settings	

Reprinted with permission from the *Advanced Product Quality Planning and Control Plan Manual and Quality System Requirements QS-9000 Manual* (Chrysler, Ford, General Motors Supplier Quality Requirements Task Force).

Typical Noncompliances in Quality Systems Audit

- No prototype control plan or prelaunch control plan found (QS-9000).
- FMEAs found without actions taken on high-risk areas (QS-9000).
- Failure to update inspection and test plans after product changes (ISO/QS-9000).
- No quality plan for low-volume product (ISO/QS-9000).
- No quality plan found for relabeled purchased product (ISO/QS-9000).
- Quality plan not developed for new water-based process line (ISO/QS-9000).
- Regrind limitations not known in molding department (ISO/QS-9000).

4.3 Contract Review

Establish and maintain documented procedures for contract review and coordination of these activities.

Guidelines for Product Safety Programs

Customers often have unique needs that include safety or regulatory requirements. Contract review involves sales, marketing, taking orders, reviewing customers' purchase orders, quoting, and up-front communications. The customer always expects to get exactly what he or she ordered, on time, and for the right price. The supplier's job is to make sure that the organization can meet the customer's requirements within the current quality program.

- Date code all sales and technical literature, advertisements, specifications, and warranties. Promptly remove obsolete materials.

- Train your sales and customer service people in processing special orders that have safety-related features. For example, some firms color code special orders or stamp them with a special designation.
- Validate all sales literature for truth in advertising. "Meets or exceeds safety standards" may not be valid unless proven by actual tests and records of ongoing tests that are kept on file.
- Establish a code of practice for the sales force that prohibits "puffing" (making promises that can't be kept or making product claims that are false).
- Terms that cannot be met need to be communicated with the customer and the order not taken until terms can be agreed upon.
- Document orders and amendments to orders and communicate them to the responsible parties. Accurate information up front is essential in order to fulfill the customers' needs.
- Retain records of contract reviews. Depending on the product retention times, these may vary. Consult your legal staff.
- Inform sales and customer service of product limitations, liability, warranty, and all aspects of consumer safety.
- Inform sales and customer service to refer technical questions to qualified staff and not to make assumptions.
- Watch for any special packaging or transport methods and note on the order. For example, shipping of certain materials may be restricted to ground transport only.
- Train all sales and customer service people in handling customer complaint and feedback procedures. Refer to 4.14.
- Educate your customers in the safest ways to use your products.

As examples of this last point, in a recent ad in *Home Safe and Sound*, Stanley Works advises its customers, "Load carefully. Before you install a Stanley hook, check out the package. It will tell you how much of a load the hook can carry. Whether you're hanging a plant or installing a swing, that can be a vital fact. There's a safe and proper way to use every one of our products. Write to..."

The Lowes Companies, Inc., is one of the top 30 retailers in the United States. It sells home improvement supplies. In 1993 it established Lowes's Home Safety Council (LHSC) as a commitment to home safety and security. In 1995, the International Public Relations Association selected LHSC to receive its Golden World Award for its community efforts. Lowes has placed "Safety Watch Kiosks" in prominent places in nearly 250 of their home improvement warehouses. The kiosks feature interactive computer screens where customers can select and view up to eight free videos on home safety topics. They also dispense safety brochures and checklists. By the year 2000, there are projected to be more than 6500 Lowes stores, and a Safety Watch Kiosk in every one.

4.4 Design Control

Control and verify the design of the product to ensure completeness in meeting specified customer requirements.

Guidelines for Product Safety Programs

Design control, and its associated functions, is one the most important elements of the quality system. The essential attributes of a product—performance, safety, and reliability—are established at the design and development phase. Safety should be built into the product at this stage, because it may be impossible to add it in later if injuries to customers result after manufacture. ISO 9000-2 and ISO 9004-1 provide additional guidance for design control.

4.4.2 Design and Development Planning

Guidelines for Product Safety Programs

- Prepare product-specific design and development plans with assigned staff responsibilities and due dates for milestones. Update the plan as the design evolves. For example, use Gant charts, market studies, and project plans.
- Assign tasks to qualified design and development staff. These may include subcontractors if used, such as finite element analysis, draftsmen, or regulatory specialists. Use input from cross-functional teams and provide technical leadership.

For example, Evenflo Juvenile Furniture Company Inc. established a development team for its award-winning Exersaucer. Consisting of marketing, quality, engineering, manufacturing, and design, the team members had one thing in common: Each was a parent of an infant. As consumers and parents, team members understood from firsthand experience what features the product needed. Evenflo uses a hazard review process team involving legal, marketing, and engineering, but also includes consumers who help analyze possible hazardous features. When the team finds hazards, like pinch points and potential for misuse, engineering designs them out of the product.

4.4.3 Organizational and Technical Interfaces

Guidelines for Product Safety Programs

- Specify cross-functional team members such as those described above in the quality manual and/or procedures.
- Organizational links and communication are extremely important in effectively implementing design control as well as design changes.

- Include external interfaces with subcontract design services, consumer groups, research consortiums, and standards development processes.

4.4.4 Design Input...Statutory and Regulatory Requirements...

Guidelines for Product Safety Programs

- Include all mandatory and voluntary product safety standards at design input.
- Resolve and clarify any unclear requirements and utilize voluntary standards and/or draft standards as they relate to potential consumer hazards.
- Include human factors as an input criterion and perform a detailed hazard analysis as part of the design failure mode effects analysis (DFMEA).

For example, the Head Impact Protection Standard for 1999 model cars calls for added protection for front and rear occupants' heads when they hit the upper vehicle components such as pillars, side rails, headers, and roofs in a crash (FMVSS #201). The National Highway Traffic Safety Administration (NHTSA) expects that compliance with this standard will prevent about 1,000 deaths and between 600 and 1,000 nonfatal head injuries each year.

Responsible and compliant firms need to obtain applicable standards and their updates. Update services are available from standards writing firms (see Appendix A). A department within your organization must be charged with keeping updates and design changes needed to stay compliant. This method of update and responsibility must be defined in your procedures. Timely review (within a matter of days) is considered best practice by QS-9000.

Many industries also monitor future standards activities to anticipate changes for cost and competitive reasons. Most large corporations volunteer staff time to participate in industry trade associations and ANSI committee work to stay abreast of developments in the standards arena. It is good practice to have your organization represented in the standards development process to keep up with the state of the art and your competition. Some companies also develop inhouse standards to exceed actual acceptance criteria found in safety standards. Often this is done to build in a safety margin to allow for some process variation and to compensate for ambiguous requirements of standards.

4.4.5 Design Output

Guidelines for Product Safety Programs

- Document that output meets input requirements. For example, use test results, field trials, dimensional layouts, safety tests, and reliability and capability studies. Early and ongoing customer feedback during the design phase reduces surprises later on.
- Document those characteristics that do not meet input criteria and specify appropriate actions such as analysis of cost/performance/risk tradeoffs, corrective actions, or alternate methods.
- Review results of hazard analysis and failure modes and effects analyses (DFMEAs) performed, including corrective actions taken.
- Specify clear acceptance criteria on prints and specifications for all characteristics of the product.
- Identify safety characteristics of the design including operating, storage, handling, maintenance, and disposal.
- Review output documents before release. For example: consumer preference tests, field trials, all safety tests, regulatory approvals, pilot build, capability studies, dimensional results, gage studies, customer approvals of drawings and specifications, quality plans, and marketing plans.

Typical Noncompliances in a Quality Systems Audit

- Test specifications found on print #7890 with no acceptance criteria for weld, warp, impact, and vibration tests.
- DFMEA found for brake hose with high-risk priority numbers and no corrective actions taken.

4.4.6 Design Review

Guidelines for Product Safety Programs

Records of design review and approval by all functions concerned are essential for feedback to the design team. Feedback for rejection of a design is also critical.

4.4.7 Design Verification

Guidelines for Product Safety Programs

- Design verification should be done by people independent of those who did the design.
- Verify that all safety characteristics and tests are documented and meet acceptance criteria.
- QS-9000 requires a comprehensive prototype program including a prototype control plan. It also requires that the same tooling and processes used in the prototype are representative of those to be used in production, where possible.

4.4.8 Design Validation

Guidelines for Product Safety Programs

Validation takes place on the final product and typically follows successful verification, but may also be necessary in earlier stages. The aim is to ensure that the product conforms to user needs and requirements. For example, Chrysler-specific requirements under

QS-9000 include annual dimensional layout to print and performance testing at least once per model year. This includes, in part, exterior lighting systems classified as safety items (FMVSS 104). In addition to the complete dimensional layout, performance testing as defined on the print specifications is required. Tests include photometrics, salt spray, vibration, moisture, dust, warpage, hot/cold cycle, aim deflection, and insulation resistance. If any failures are found, corrective action is required. The following is a design validation and design change case study.

Binney & Smith, Inc., makers of Crayola Crayons, launched food-scented crayons in January 1994. Acknowledging that the crayons were in total compliance with all the safety and regulatory laws, officials were concerned that food-scented crayons would increase the likelihood of a child-choking hazard risk (although there had been not a single incident of ingestion reported). Binney & Smith made a quick decision, based on consumer statements and opinions of child safety advocates, to phase out their biggest-selling product, new food-scented Crayolas.

By mid-September, Binney & Smith advised the United States Consumer Product Safety Commission of its intention, and developed a new line of nonfood-scented Crayolas. In April 1995 new Majic Scent crayons were offered with floral scents (lilac, eucalyptus) and nonfloral scents (new car, soap, leather, cedar, lumber, baby powder, and dirt). CEO Richard S. Gurin remarked, "Even at a cost well in excess of a half million dollars to develop and phase in the new scents into our production, we feel it was a good idea to preserve the reputation of the Crayola brand for safety."

4.4.9 Design Changes

Guidelines for Product Safety Programs

- Develop an engineering change procedure with a log or tracking mechanism.

- Notify all functions concerned so that adjustments can be made to inventory, gages, procedures, tooling, materials, packaging, and inspection instructions, prior to the actual change. Institute a documented system for this procedure, such as an Engineering Change Notice (ECN).
- Notify customers of change for written approval (QS-9000 PPAP). Many automotive recalls result from suppliers who make unapproved changes without notifying their customers. Examples include: using an inferior grade of plastic as a temporary substitute for a high-strength application; use of an incompatible lubricant as a temporary fix.
- Require review and approval by authorized staff for all changes. Require supporting data to validate that the change is required and follow up. This calls for a quality record. Many firms use a cross-functional sign-off process to assure communication.

Typical Noncompliances in a Quality Systems Audit

- Design review for product "X" not signed off by all functions specified in the procedure.
- Design validation not found for servodrives.
- Dimensional change found on print for engineering change initiated nine months prior; no follow-up.
- Warning labels and location not specified for rotary mixer.
- Software for knurling machine not current or validated for emergency stop.
- Design output does not meet input criteria: Vibration test and algorithm scan 5 to 75 degrees horizontal exceeds specification limits with no corrective action.
- Warning and maintenance manuals not kept current with design changes.

- Four of five development plans behind schedule in excess of three months; four design staff members have recently been terminated.
- Drafting standards not current with ANSI Geometric Dimensional Tolerancing Standard. Primary datum is not specified on drawing.

Product Recall Preventable Through 4.4 (Design Control)

- **Fuel filler spouts and vents.** Problem: Fuel overflows when vehicles are full of gasoline and parked on a hill, causing potential fire hazard.
- **Miniature Christmas tree lights.** Problem: Undersized wiring, a low melting point for decorative holders, lack of fuse, and polarized plug may present a potential fire hazard.
- **Bike helmets.** Problem: Helmet liners failed the manufacturer's head-impact tests and may not prevent injuries.
- **Baby float.** Problem: A child sitting in the device could drown if water leaks into the hollow center of the float's inner tube, causing the device to tip over.
- **Cleaner.** Problem: The product, which contains high levels of sodium hydroxide, was not packaged in accordance with the Federal Hazardous Substances Act.
- **Lawn torches.** Problem: Torches may suddenly erupt, shooting flames and hot wax.
- **Coffeemakers.** Problem: About 750,000 coffeemakers sold contain thermostats that could present a fire hazard.
- **Pacifiers.** Problem: Pacifiers fail regulation requiring venting holes to prevent small children from suffocating.
- **Car.** Problem: Flexible brake-line hoses fail to meet safety standards and could cause loss of brakes.
- **Machine.** Problem: Controller software and defective controller may cause machine to not follow shutdown sequence, which may cause injury to the operator.
- **Battery.** Problem: Defective model may explode and cause serious injury to user.

- **Van.** Problem: Transmission may slip into neutral from park, causing hazard to pedestrians.

4.5 Document and Data Control

Control all documents and data related to quality.

Refer to Figure 5.4.

Figure 5.4
Quality System Documentation Progression

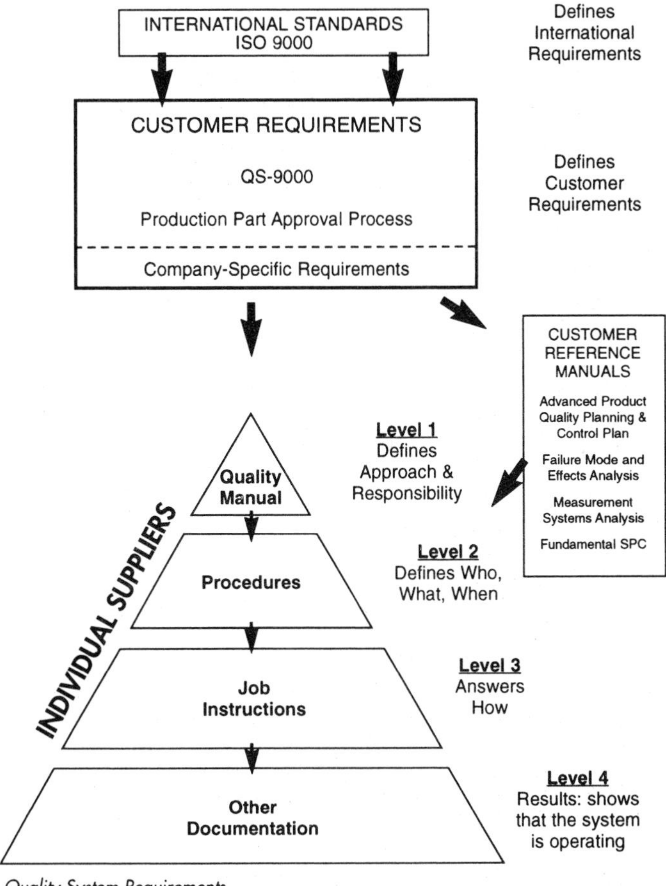

Quality System Requirements

Reprinted with permission from the *Advanced Product Quality Planning and Control Plan Manual and Quality System Requirements: QS-9000 Manual* (Chrysler, Ford, General Motors Supplier Quality Requirement Task Force).

Guidelines for Product Safety Programs

In order to consistently produce safe products, the management system must have methods to control all documents and data relating to product quality. Standards, customer drawings, and electronic media are specified by the standards. This element is typically difficult to comply with because of the volume of data generated in a quality program.

Documents are not only essential to control the process, but they become important in litigation. A list of required documents in a product liability action may include engineering drawings, product specifications, test reports, design reviews, product brochures, warranties, manuals, installation instructions, sales and purchase orders, and copies of warnings attached to the product and shipping records. The list may grow more extensive as the litigation presses on.

Better and faster access to information is a key strategy for maintaining product safety, reliability, and quality.

- Establish procedures for control of drawings, specifications, procedures, work instructions/forms and process setup sheets.
- Mark process control guidelines and similar documents with customer's "special characteristics" symbol to indicate that step in the process or that product characteristic that has safety-related or special significance (QS-9000).
- Include electronic data control methods for test software, test results, master lists, math data, and records. For example: password protection, backup methods, read-only access, storage, and disaster recovery for computer systems.
- Use master lists for drawings, external and internal specifications, procedures, and work instructions. For example, use an electronic database to keep the customer drawing master list, ensuring that only the latest is used.
- Subscribe to ASTM, ANSI, ISO, Boise Cascade, GM, Ford, Chrysler, U.S. Federal Register, Japanese Industrial

Standards, Canadian Standards Association, and any required standards publisher for updates to stay current with the most recent customer standards. Assign responsibility for review and distribution. Typically, the index volume serves as a master list with latest revision dates. Contact your customers for specification updates resulting from standards changes on a scheduled basis if no update service is available.

4.5.2 Document and Data Approval and Issue

Guidelines for Product Safety Programs

- Review, approve, and date all documents prior to issue.
- Keep applicable and/or visual standards controlled copies at or near work sites.

For example, one molding company uses representative samples as visual instructions for its machine operators. A board with the samples is posted in the molding area. The samples are marked specifically with acceptance criteria, date, and approval of the QA inspector, as specified in the company's procedures. All operators interviewed were well aware of product quality standards, as well as the visual acceptance criteria.

4.5.3 Document and Data Changes

Guidelines for Product Safety Programs

- Establish who can make changes.
- Make decisions for change based on data, and have background data available.
- Identify the nature of the change in the document or attachment. For example, the revision history in the quality manual and changes can be marked with an asterisk. Or a revision block on a drawing can specify which dimension or characteristic has changed.

Typical Noncompliances in a Quality Systems Audit

- Engineering specifications found not current with index.
- FMVSS and SAE specifications found in use at lab are not up to date.
- Obsolete prints found in machining area; products being produced to these prints.
- Blending procedure found in molding area with no date or approval.
- MIS procedure found in use for data backup and storage with no date or approval.
- Visual reference sample of conforming printed circuit board with no date or authorization.
- Obsolete manufacturing specification found in use calling for Type Xe lubricant, which was phased out for product failure. Xe lubricant is still used.

4.6 Purchasing

Control purchased products and services, subcontractors, and suppliers to ensure that they meet specifications.

Guidelines for Product Safety Programs

Purchasing operations are vital to the effective performance of the quality system, ensuring safety of the end product, as well as contributing to accident reduction. An actual example of the problems a supplier can cause was experienced by a manufacturer when the supplier of a tuning assembly changed the epoxy encapsulating process without notifying the customer, who assembles the device. Out-gassing from the new epoxy corroded a relay contact, causing a short circuit and fire.

QS-9000 states, "All materials used in part manufacture shall satisfy...safety constraints...restricted, toxic, and hazardous materials; as well as environmental, electrical, and electromagnetic considerations...."

This requirement is specific to the automotive industry. It requires you to have data available for the materials you purchase relative to Material Safety Data Sheets (MSDSs) and Certificates of Conformity regardless of the country of manufacture and sale. Restricted substance specifications (PCBs, cadmium, dioxin) can be found within the engineering standards volumes of the Big Three, often as a print specification. This requirement is also a part of the PPAP process. It is important to note that even sample materials should be ordered with the above information, so that the design function can evaluate the material against the requirements.

- Develop and maintain procedures for purchasing activities to ensure your purchased materials comply with specified requirements.
- Identify all safety-related considerations for suppliers and purchasing to include in the procedures, such as:
  - Departmental interfaces
  - Availability of accident data and recalls
  - Timely vendor performance data
  - Feedback and corrective action loop
  - MSDS and compatibility with plant needs
  - Material substitution for less hazardous substances
  - Bill of material accuracy
  - Knowledge of product safety specifications, codes, standards, and regulations
  - Access to plant safety procedures such as safe lifting and contractor safety

4.6.2 Evaluation of Subcontractors

- Establish acceptance criteria for qualified suppliers. Ensure that acceptance criteria allow purchasing agents to pass up low price quotations from suppliers with unacceptable safety and quality records.

- Maintain an approved supplier list (records) procedure; add new suppliers and delete unsatisfactory suppliers as needed.
- Define how you will ensure evaluation of all purchased materials and services (and suppliers) that affect product quality and safety. For example, calibration, test, and design services often affect product quality and safety. Typical materials other than standard production materials that are often overlooked on the approved supplier list include: repair materials, certain types of packaging, resale products, and certain types of safety-related transport.
- Tell your subcontractors on your purchase orders that they must notify you of design and process changes and indicate their compliance with QS-9000 and PPAP.
- Establish a feedback and corrective action loop for non-conforming shipments and audits. Maintain records of these.

A Case History Example: Toys "R" Us

Toys "R" Us implemented a safety assurance program that emphasized vendor awareness of new and evolving regulations and standards, and keeping potentially hazardous products from the shelves and hands of customers. Toys "R" Us elected to classify all products into two major categories: toys that pose a high risk of hazard, and toys that pose a low risk of hazard.

It defined high-risk toys as those intended for children from birth through 36 months. All high-risk toys are tested prior to every shipment made. Low-risk toys are generally defined as those intended for children 37 months and older. These are tested once every calendar year prior to shipping. Testing is performed by an approved, qualified testing laboratory that Toys "R" Us chose as its program partner in 1989.

In 1991, Toys "R" Us created customized systems and computer programs to allow constant monitoring of the flow of product through the testing process. The system analyzed the results of every product and vendor test. A safeguard in the cash register system prevents recalled products from being sold accidentally. The computer pricing system controlled by the inventory department sets the price at $9,999 for any recalled product. If by chance, store personnel miss an item that has been identified as hazardous or that has been recalled, a customer trying to buy it would be faced with a price of almost $10,000, and the register clerk would be able to capture the item.

Additionally, quarterly and annual recaps are done on each vendor's performance. Poor performing vendors are advised of their status and dealt with accordingly. The safety assurance program has increased its scope and expanded its original goals. A corporate safety committee meets quarterly to discuss safety and compliance issues that reach beyond the basics of just testing products.

A key event each year is the schedule of safety seminars for buyers. Safety-related information based on each buyer's categories is presented, as is a general overview for the newest members of the buying staff. Staff members are brought up to date on the latest issues in their categories, testing data, CPSC recalls, and vendor performance.

Toys "R" Us also sponsors an annual vendor seminar. Suppliers learn of any recent developments in the safety area, review the provisions and requirements of the Toys "R" Us program, and discuss any other topics relative to toy safety.

4.6.3 Purchasing Data

Guidelines for Product Safety Programs

- Specify clearly data that describe the product on the purchase order. Include part number, exact description, and revision level of the drawing or specification. This may also include MSDS and a certificate of compliance with every shipment, quantity, delivery date/time, or any other critical characteristic depending on the product or service ordered.

- The buyer or authorized designate should require review and approval of all relevant data prior to release.
- Clearly specify title, number, and quality system standard to be applied.

4.6.4 Verification of Purchased Product

Guidelines for Product Safety Programs

- Specify on the purchase order if source inspections at your supplier's manufacturing site are required. For example, a machinery manufacturer must allow its customer's safety engineer access to its plant to perform a required safety inspection on a production machine prior to shipment. This requirement was specified on the purchase order.
- When nonconforming purchased parts or materials are discovered, purchasing should be promptly notified so that corrective action can be expedited by the supplier. In some cases product recall may be necessary to prevent injury to consumers.

Preventable Product Recalls Through Proper Purchasing Methods

- A design service prepares drawings for a machine, and the electrical schematic was drawn incorrectly resulting in electrocution of a temporary worker. It was later determined that the design firm had no electrical engineer or electrician for review of the prints.
- Repair of ladders was performed as a rework operation. Substandard bolts were used. Whereas the grade was the same as production bolts, the repair operation used bolts from an unapproved source.
- An unapproved calibration service was used to calibrate high-voltage electrical testers. It was later found that the equipment used to calibrate the high-voltage testers was in error. The product tested by the high-voltage tester had to be recalled.

Typical Noncompliances in a Quality Systems Audit

- Epoxy material found at a rework station. Supplier of the epoxy is not an approved supplier.
- Purchase order does not specify revision of drawing, as required in procedures.
- No corrective action response found for rejected shipments, and no evidence that the supplier was notified of nonconforming safety-related shipments.
- Supplier's receiving inspection performance criteria is set at 10 rejected shipments. After 12 rejected shipments, no action is taken to disqualify or find another source as indicated by the procedure.
- Approved supplier list not kept up to date as required by internal procedures.
- Supplier audit report found on supplier of brake components, with no corrective action response found.

4.7 Control of Customer-Supplied Product

Control verification, storage, and maintenance of products supplied by customers.

Guidelines for Product Safety Programs

- Customer-owned product/materials may be used to manufacture end products or in service applications. Safety-related issues need consideration for this element as it applies to your operation.
- Develop a procedure to handle customer-supplied product. This may be as simple as referencing existing procedure for receiving, handling, and identifying product, and for nonconforming product.
- Keep records of receipt, inspection, and customer notification.

- Report loss or damage to the customer in a timely manner. For example, QS-9000 automotive requirements specify that the customer shall provide returnable packaging and tooling for this element. However, this could also be production materials, test devices, or other items that are used in manufacture or service applications.

4.8 Product Identification and Traceability

Establish and maintain a system for tracing the product at all stages from receipt of raw material to installation, servicing, and disposal.

Guidelines for Product Safety Programs

Proper identification and traceability of materials and product are required to prevent inadvertent use of the wrong material and mix-ups during all stages from receipt through delivery and installation. They also help in identification of nonconforming product that may have been produced using nonconforming raw materials. Lot traceability from finished goods to raw materials may be required, depending on your industry, customer requirements, and regulations.

- Establish your traceability procedures based on regulatory and customer requirements and known best practice for your industry type. Examples: The U.S. Food and Drug Administration regulates product and utilizes Good Manufacturing Practices (GMPs) for certain traceability requirements. Pharmaceuticals require traceability from the raw materials to the finished product and from the finished product back to the raw materials. This requires batches or lots to have unique identification codes. The EPA requires registration of sanitizers by both their trade names and chemical names. The Federal Insecticide, Fungicide, and Rodenticide Act (FIFRA) requires specific label information and technical literature. Disinfectants must be identified by the phrase, "It is a violation of federal law to use this product in a manner inconsistent with its labeling."

- Use labels, tags, bins, areas, inventory systems, stamps, routers, or some form of identification for all production materials. Define these specific methods in your procedures.
- Identification of some bulk processes may be accomplished through a record of times, flow rates, and location. Use of tags may be physically impossible.

Determine the need for lot traceability and utilize logs, routers, tags, and/or some combination of the methods to achieve traceability. For example, QS-9000 Traceability from finished product to raw materials is typically specified as part-specific and is called out on the drawing. Certain key processes such as heat treating require lot traceability as specified in the Ford requirements.

Typical Noncompliances in a Quality Systems Audit

- Federal Motor Vehicle Safety Standards (FMVSS) lot traceability to raw material not found as specified (PF Safety) on print. FMVSS item.
- Four of 10 bins of fasteners found in the assembly area with no label.
- In-process product found at the welding area is missing the last operation on the tag.
- Retained samples of material for four of five lots not found as specified in the procedure.
- Lot date and revision level are not found on the label as specified in the procedure.
- Acrylic regrind not labeled. Found in use in the molding area; the process sheet does not specify use of regrind material.

Preventable Product Recall Through Product Identification and Traceability

- Rotary centrifuge. Problem: A nonhardened spring was inadvertently mixed up with the hardened springs in the assembly operations. Product fails at high speeds, causing potential injury from projectiles and debris.

4.9 Process Control

Identify and plan the manufacturing process to assure that it is carried out under controlled conditions.

Guidelines for Product Safety Programs

This element defines the requirements to manage and control production and manufacturing systems. Preventing problems by controlling the process is the objective, as opposed to detecting problems at the final inspection or operation. Inadequate process controls contribute to production defects and noncompliances even with a proven "safe design" product.

4.9(c) Compliance with Standards/Codes

This section requires your firm to take responsible actions for ensuring the safety of your products and services during production, servicing, and installation, even if your firm is not responsible for the design. Compliance with standards/ codes is essential. Customer-specified requirements must also be met, including those that might affect a product's safety, compliance with government regulations, fit, function, or quality of subsequent manufacturing operations.

- Plan for process controls prior to production. Use cross-functional teams for process planning; include tools such as process FMEAs, pilot builds, advance manufacturing trials, preliminary process capability studies, correlation testing, and early customer inputs where possible.
- Document, approve, and maintain precise and up-to-date procedures and work instructions, photographs, illustrations, and/or representative samples. Examples: process sheets, manufacturing specifications, bills of material, routing sheets, packing instructions, drawings, control plans, inspection plans, maintenance checklists, and test instructions.

- Include within work instructions:
  - — Procedures for what to do if the process goes out of control
  - — Clear acceptance criteria for product
  - — Environmental conditions
  - — Special handling
  - — Labeling
  - — Frequency of process checks
  - — Materials/quantities
  - — Ranges for process parameters
- Do not overlook clear acceptance criteria. Operators must know good from nonconforming parts and what to do with nonconforming parts to keep them isolated from the process.
- Date and approve representative samples and photographs.
- Design your processes to prevent nonconforming products by using fail-safe methods and Poka Yokes (see Appendix E for the Shingo Shigeo text). Examples: Use computer systems with closed-loop controls, sensors, analyzers, alarms, and measurement equipment.

Vision-equipped robots make sense for process control where human eyes are deficient. A computer factory in California inserts a 256K RAM chip into a circuit board, and a vision device under the board checks all the leads to make sure that each is bent at a 90° angle.

An automotive supplier in the Midwest uses fail-safe sensors in its robotic welders to prevent missing welds and fasteners. The sensors are checked daily for proper function. Shingo Shigeo's Poka Yoke book illustrates many mistake-proofing devices: positive locators, fixtures, and jigs that prevent human error and other process variation.

- Monitor process parameters and product characteristics at the specified frequency, and record verifications, inspections, and/or tests. Example: A supplier of automotive exterior lighting systems monitors retroreflection of tail lamp lenses in its molding area. This characteristic is a safety item (MVSS 104) and is found marked as such on the control plan. Lenses are checked hourly: one right and one left of each cavity. The legal requirement states that only right-hand assemblies need testing. This company checks both sides for reflectance.
- Establish preventive maintenance: Include predictive methods, perishable tooling, computer software (test or process), test/measurement and processing equipment, and proper cleaning and lubrication. Examples: Some firms use PM software to schedule and have specific checklists for each type of equipment. Checklists are typically based on equipment manuals and safety regulations, but may also be keyed to a specific product characteristic. Consider using operator PM checklists for general maintenance, and a more involved checklist for the maintenance department. Smaller firms sometimes use a wall-matrix–type schedule that serves as both a scheduling tool and a record. This method is not as paper-intensive as some computer methods that are used, but can be just as effective.
- Keep records of process changes and notify your customers when required (QS-9000 PPAP).
- It is imperative to keep a history of actual repairs, as well as preventive work. Tooling management systems generally use cycle-count frequency scheduling, tagging of tooling, and last-off part methods for tool and die repairs.

QS-9000 requires several additional steps in process control:

- 4.9.3 Ongoing Process Control A CpK >= 1.33 and a PpK >= 1.67, and customer-specific reaction plans for containment of process output and 100 percent inspection.
- 4.9.4 Modified Preliminary or Ongoing Capability Requirements.

- 4.9.5 Verification of Job Setups. (This is typically a first piece type inspection.)
- 4.9.6 Process Changes. A record of process changes and prior customer approval (PPAP) is required for change in part number, manufacturing location, material sources, and production process environment. Suppliers must maintain a record of process change dates and effective dates.

Figure 5.5 is a Ford-specific requirement for containment of suspect product and corrective actions when a process or product control chart has gone out of control.

Figure 5.5
Ongoing Process and Product Monitoring: Control Chart Interpretation and Reaction (Ford Specific)

The MOST RECENT POINT indicates that the process:	**ACTIONS ON THE PROCESS OUTPUT Based on the Historical Process Capability (Cpk)**		
	Less than 1.33*	1.33 – 1.67	Greater than 1.67
Is in control	100% inspect	Accept product. Continue to reduce product variation.	
Has gone out of control in an adverse direction. All individuals in the sample are within specification.	100% inspect	**IDENTIFY AND CORRECT SPECIAL CAUSE** Inspect 100% since the last in-control point.	Accept product. Continue to reduce process variation.
Has gone out of control and one or more individuals in the sample are outside specification.	100% inspect	**IDENTIFY AND CORRECT SPECIAL CAUSE** 100% inspect product produced since the last in-control sample.	

*Unless superseded by a Control Plan.

This table applies only when stability and capability have been demonstrated and special causes are rigorously identified and eliminated. Otherwise, 100% inspection is required. The table applies only to those product characteristics that are normally distributed.

Source: Reprinted with permission from the *Advanced Product Quality Planning and Control Plan Manual* and *Quality System Requirements: QS-9000 Manual* (Chrysler, Ford, General Motors Supplier Quality Requirements Task Force).

Typical Noncompliances in a Quality Systems Audit

- No part weight check performed as specified in the quality plan for foamed ABS.
- Clean room procedure specifies "no cardboard": cardboard boxes found in the clean room.
- Inspection plan calls for 100 percent high-voltage electrical check: only every tenth unit checked by second shift.
- Machine (product) found with no instruction for warning labels, per ANSI specification and customer purchase order.
- Acceptance criteria not specified for weld depth penetration on weld operation 20.
- Progressive die preventive maintenance schedule is due at 100,000 cycles. Actual cycle count is at 450,000 with no actual maintenance done.

Preventable Product Recalls

A furniture maker's chair seat post may unexpectedly separate from the base, causing the chair to fall over. Seven reports were cited. Nearly 150,000 desk chairs were recalled by the CPSC. Weld failures due to lack of process control are a suspected cause.

A children's sleepwear firm agreed to pay $110,000 to settle allegations that it violated CPSC standards for the flammability of the product. It is reported that the company used piping on some of the garments without proper testing or record keeping. The CPSC also alleged that the firm continued to sell flammable sleepwear after it was notified of the violations.

4.10 Inspection and Testing

Establish and carry out procedures for testing to ensure that product meets quality specifications.

Guidelines for Product Safety Programs

This element covers receiving, in-process, and final inspection and testing. Sampling plans are an essential part of most systems. Safety-related items typically require tests more often than for nonsafety-related items or products. The use of receiving and in-process inspections should not be overlooked as a method for preventing and minimizing nonconformities and production defects.

- Establish and document inspection and test procedures.
- Include frequency, sample size, how to inspect against the quality plan, equipment/gage specific instructions, data to record, how to mark product or tag, and what to do in the event of failure.
- Include a statement saying falsification of data is not acceptable. The person making the entry may be accountable for the results of the test. Firms and individuals have been fined and sentenced to jail terms for falsifying data.

4.10.2 Receiving Inspection and Testing

- Ensure that no items are used until their fitness for use has been verified against the quality plan.
- Clearly mark areas for hold, quarantine, and nonconforming parts. Have an additional tagging or marking system in place as a backup. Hold areas are typically the first to be filled to overcapacity. A combination of tagging and a secure hold area seems to be the most effective.

- Equip your receiving staff with properly calibrated tools and equipment. In some cases, scales are used in shipping and receiving for part counts, weight verifications, and maximum loading capacity for trucks. Do not overlook calibration for scales!
- Plan to what extent testing will be performed for receiving and who is authorized to change levels of inspection.
- Record inspection data, including lot number for traceability where applicable.
- Review certificates of conformity. Mark status of items as required in your procedures. Examples: QS-9000 Ford-specific requirements cite "Control Item Fasteners," which require traceability. This starts in receiving and needs to be recorded.

4.10.3 In-Process Inspection and Testing

Guidelines for Product Safety Programs

- Perform in-process inspections against the quality plan and record the results. Examples: In-process tests and inspections may include setup and first piece inspection, inspection by operators, automatic tests, fixed inspection intervals, patrol inspections, and SPC applications.
- Do not allow the product to move to the next operation until verified as acceptable.
- Specify what actions are to be taken if out-of-control process conditions are found: where a nonconforming product should be placed, how to identify it, containment of nonconforming product, and how to record SPC charts (circle out-of-control points and note actions taken).

4.10.4 Final Inspection and Test

Guidelines for Product Safety Programs

Safety-related products require higher levels of assurance than nonsafety-related products. Acceptance tests are required at either 100 percent, lot sampling, and/or continuous sampling methods. The CPSC reports that reworked components of finished products are often a source of product failure. Extreme caution is advised in this area (refer to 4.13 Control of Nonconforming Product).

- No product should be shipped until all specified tests in the quality plan are satisfactorily completed and recorded.
- It is essential to use properly calibrated equipment, documented test methods, and clear acceptance criteria. Example: A consumer electronics firm tests 100 percent of product for current leakage. The requirement is specified in an ANSI/UL spec on the customer's print. An audit found that a loose connector allowed the ground wire to disconnect during or prior to the test, causing a "pass" reading without energizing the product. Although the operator had asked for repair several days before, nonconforming parts were allowed to pass the test. Faulty and operator-sensitive equipment may allow nonconforming and defective product to be shipped. Mistake-proof your test equipment! (Refer to 4.11.)

4.10.5 Inspection and Test Records

Guidelines for Product Safety Programs

- Records must clearly show whether the product has passed or failed, and who performed the test or inspection.
- Retain and collect all test and inspection records for your legal requirements and record retention system.

- Retain scrap, repair, and reinspection records to prove corrective action and disposition of nonconforming products.
- Perform QS-9000 layout inspection and functional testing. For example, Chrysler-specific requirements cite an annual frequency for complete layout inspection and design validation/product verification. (Exceptions require written concurrence from Chrysler.)
- Outside laboratories should be qualified and found in your approved supplier records, as their services affect the quality and safety of your product.

Typical Noncompliances in a Quality Systems Audit

- 4.10.2 Sampling plan not used in receiving inspection per quality plan. Receiving checks only three parts per shipment, based on interviews and records.
- 4.10.3 In-process testing per the control plan specifies one part, each cavity, per hour to be checked for flatness. Operator checks one part per hour but does not check all four cavities.
- 4.10.4 Continuity check performed at the final assembly is not found in the quality plan. Also, no record is kept.
- 4.10.5 Record found for weld test does not clearly specify pass or fail. Also inspector's initials not found for September 1995 on the record.
- 4.10.5 No test records found to validate sales literature for FMVSS 302 flammability for styrene resin.

Preventable Product Recall Through Proper Inspection and Testing Methods

Infant carrier. Problem: Some of the white plastic handles may break, causing the infant to fall. The production error may be due to lack of instructions and use of the wrong type of plastic.

4.11 Control of Inspection, Measuring, and Test Equipment

Establish and maintain procedures to control, calibrate, and maintain test and measurement equipment.

Guidelines for Product Safety Programs

This element applies to equipment used in verifying product quality. This process covers all aspects in the product life cycle, from development through repair and disposal. It is helpful to think of the measurement system as a process involving materials, equipment, procedures, and people. Measurement systems for testing, measuring, and inspecting safety items require rigorous control and safe-proofs to assure reliability of data. Additional guidance for this element is covered in ISO 10012.

- Establish and maintain procedures for calibration of all types of test equipment. Use equipment manuals or ask the manufacturer to provide a calibration procedure. Another source of calibration procedures is to contact your outside supplier of calibration services for its procedures as a starting point.
- Ensure that the equipment is sufficiently accurate to properly measure the process and the product. Consider a 10:1 accuracy ratio as a starting point: The device should be precise enough to measure a tolerance one-tenth of the dimension to be measured. For example, if the tolerance of a part dimension is ±0.001, the test device should be accurate to ±0.0001.
- Calculate the measurement uncertainty so that the known measurement uncertainty is consistent with the required measurement capability.
- Use a 10:1 or 4:1 accuracy ratio (i.e., calibration device to the measurement device), and a gage repeatability and reproducibility study to determine whether the measurement process itself is in a state of statistical control. See *Military Handbook 95B,* and *MIL STD 45662A*, for additional data on accuracy ratios. Extremely high-resolution

equipment and instrumentation clusters may require considerable uncertainty calculations due to tolerance stack up and other factors.

- Include all test software and hardware involved in the measurement system, so that these items can be checked to prove they are capable of verifying the acceptability of product. For example, test software is used in qualifying an electrohydraulic device on an automated assembly line. The test stand is checked daily with a known failure to verify proper functioning. This daily check is documented, in addition to the annual calibration against a NIST traceable reference standard.
- Establish a scheduled recall system for all calibrations and a method to identify the calibration status of all Measurement and Test Equipment (M&TE). Typically, a calibration sticker is used.
- Keep records of all calibrations, and include acceptance criteria, NIST traceability, unique identification of the M&TE, and actual readings of the "as received" M&TE when out-of-tolerance conditions are discovered.
- Where M&TE are found to be out of calibration, assess previous test results for possible shipment or production of nonconforming product. This may necessitate customer notification or a product recall. For example, a calibration report found an out-of-tolerance condition on a torque wrench. It was reading 2 foot-pounds below its acceptance criteria. A review of the product tests performed by the torque wrench for the past six months (date of its last calibration) showed all passing results in excess of 4 foot-pounds, so that the calibration error was small enough not to create a problem situation. The torque wrench was dedicated to this product line, so the conclusion was that no conconforming product was produced even with the faulty calibration. However, the calibration frequency was subsequently increased from six months to three months.
- Specify environmental conditions that apply to performing calibrations. Examples include temperature, humidi-

ty, particulates, and power conditioners to prevent electrical spikes and brownouts.

- Preserve and store reference standards that have a shelf life; check for expiration dates and replace as needed. Examples: pH buffers, viscosity standards, oils, and biological media.
- Protect portable test equipment from damage and misuse. Examples include shock mounts, protective cases, and restrictions regarding use.
- Establish storage methods to prevent contamination, damage, and deterioration of reference standards and M&TE. For example, dimensional gage blocks should be stored in their protective case to prevent inadvertent use. If stored in a corrosive environment, they may rust, causing inaccuracy.
- Safeguard test equipment. Watch for adjustments that could invalidate the calibration setting. For example, tamperproof seals and interlocks are often used on adjustments for meters and electrical testers. Password protection on test software is often used as a mistake proof. A typical safeguard used to verify in-line testers is simply a known bad part, as a daily or per shift recorded check. Even sensors fail!
- Outside calibration subcontractors should be considered suppliers, and qualified as an approved supplier prior to use. After all, their work has a direct impact on the quality of your products. Request a sample certificate prior to placing an order, along with a copy of their quality manual.
- Review calibration reports to ensure valid and complete data are recorded. Some calibration labs will charge extra for as-found readings and NIST traceability. You may have to make explicit purchase order requirements to get consistency if you use numerous calibration suppliers.
- QS-9000 requires conformance to methods specified in the Automotive Industry Action Group's *Measurement Systems Analysis* reference manual.

Typical Noncompliances in a Quality Systems Audit

- Calibration report found for a flowmeter with no acceptance criteria specified.
- Out-of-tolerance power supply calibration report; no evidence of assessment of previous test results.
- Numerous gages found in the assembly area with no calibration status.
- Voltmeter used to test product with adjustment port, and no safeguard.
- Scales found in the shipping department for part count are not calibrated.
- Rockwell hardness block found in use with more indentations than allowed in the ASTM standard for hardness testing.

4.12 Inspection and Test Status

Identify the inspection and test status of all product pertaining to conformance or nonconformance.

Guidelines for Product Safety Programs

Clear identification of test or inspection status is required for all product to ensure that only acceptable product is used. This applies to purchased materials, in-process product, and finished goods. Although this element allows flexibility in what methods are used, it is essential that a product's status is known at all times. Refer to Figure 5.6. This includes status categories such as "not yet tested," "awaiting results," "passed," or "failed." For safety-related product items, the accuracy of this status could be a matter of life or death.

- Develop and maintain procedures that cover all aspects of your operations. For example, although tags apply to the assembly area, a designated area labeled "hold" may be required for in-process work in the welding depart-

Figure 5.6
Inspection and Test Status Flow Chart

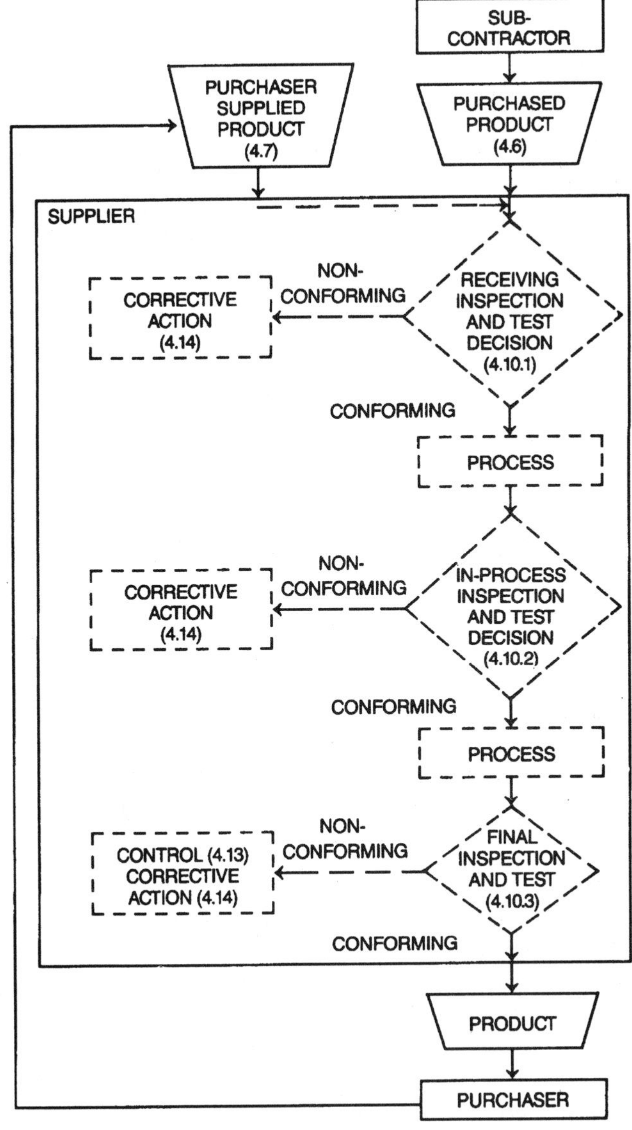

Source: *ANSI/ASQC Q90 and ISO 9000 Guidelines for Use by the Chemical and Process Industries,* 1992, ASQC, p.71. Reprinted with permission by the American Society for Quality Control.

ment. In the finished goods area, a computerized hold mechanism can be employed.

- Specify all types of status verification and their respective areas in the procedure.

4.13 Control of Nonconforming Product

Systems should be in place to ensure that all product that does not conform to specifications is not used or installed.

Guidelines for Product Safety Programs

The steps for dealing with nonconforming product must be established and maintained in documented procedures. The objective is to prevent the customer from receiving any unsafe or nonconforming product. It is desirable to produce a highly visual effect in the identification of nonconforming product. Make nonconforming and suspect product "stick out like a sore thumb." Track and develop a prioritized plan to reduce repair, rework, and scrap.

- Clearly identify all suspect and nonconforming material using the methods specified in your procedure.
- Set up controls to monitor third-party disposal and repair operations. For example, a network of discount stores and a manufacturer of consumer goods took a lesson in nonconforming identification the hard way. A batch of electric frying pans with defective heating elements was handed over to a disposal firm for destruction. Instead, the firm sold the frying pans to a discount retailer as being seconds because of cosmetic imperfections. The manufacturer first realized what happened when customer complaints began flowing in.
- Set up a review by designated persons to determine whether nonconforming product can be repaired, reworked, regraded, accepted by concession, or scrapped. Persons carrying out this review must be competent, to evaluate the effects of the decision relative to fitness for use and safety.

- Adequately stock your operations with red bins, tags, markers, or whatever means your procedure specifies.
- According to the CPSC, repair and rework of safety-related product carries more risk than scrapping. For example, an electric heater is rejected for failing the high-voltage test. It is tagged and sent to repair. The heating element is replaced as specified in the repair procedure. It is then retested for the high-voltage test and passes. The repair person notes that sometimes a heater comes in for repair *without any description of the nonconformance.* As a matter of practice the repair person has done his or her best to fix any and all problems. This is a noncompliance and is a potential hazard relative to product safety.
- Repair and rework instructions must be described in writing, and in detail.
- Retest and inspect against the quality plan.
- To facilitate possible recalls, final inspection and test records must note repair details, serial/lot numbers, repair person, and inspector. For example, a batch of toasters was reworked over a period of a month. In that time a new supplier's switch was phased in. The switch failed in use and the manufacturer recalled all items from the same batch. Twice as many toasters as expected poured in, because the reworked toasters shared the same lot number, although they carried the old switch.
- Recall unsafe, nonconforming product whether in finished goods, in transit, or already in use.
- Take appropriate actions to eliminate the causes of the nonconformities, and to avoid recurrence. Reduce waste and variation; focus on preventing the causes of nonconforming material. See Shingo Shigeo's Poka Yoke, Appendix E.

Typical Noncompliances in a Quality Systems Audit

- Numerous baskets of nonconforming material found in slitting department, not identified as such, per procedure.

- Rejected suction plates found in nonconforming area. Tag is missing "description" of nonconformity per procedure.
- Repaired disposition records reviewed, 6 of 10 show no evidence of retest.
- Found repair operation on wheel cylinder line; no documented repair instructions.
- Torque wrench found on rework bench; no evidence of calibration.
- Quality manual specifies material review board as responsible for disposition. Disposition actually performed by inspector.

4.14 Corrective and Preventive Action

Actions shall be taken and documented to correct or prevent product nonconformities on the basis of customer complaints and other sources of information.

Guidelines for Product Safety Programs

Establish and maintain procedures for rapid response where customer complaints involve product safety issues. Include actions taken to noncompliances in your internal audits, complaints both internal and external, and any other source of problematic concerns to the quality system.

- Keep a record of all customer complaints.
- Assign responsibility for corrective action and target dates for closure.

Investigate and record the cause of the problem. The CPSC reports that Playskool molds their toll-free number into all of its products to let parents know its people are there when they need them. All of Playskool's product packaging features innovative "ages and stages" icons. The system helps take the guesswork out of choosing toys by organizing them into stages of development: newborn, infant, toddler, and preschool.

"The most important thing if you have a problem is to nip it in the bud, so that way it stays a small problem. Don't be indecisive—move on it right away," says Alan Hassenfeld, Chairman and Chief Executive Officer of Hasbro, speaking at the 1995 CPSC Safety Sells Conference.

- Determine who in your company must be involved, what their roles are, how to coordinate those functions, and what steps each must follow should a consumer safety issue arise.
- Define your process for consumer safety issues, whether in marketing, communications, consumer affairs, quality, or engineering to take appropriate actions immediately upon alert. For example, Whirlpool's continual monitoring of and contact with consumers provide data to mount such alerts if a safety issue arises. Concerns may surface from a variety of sources including testing, the service network, distribution, or the consumer "1-800" number. Any consumer complaint targeting potential safety issues that arrives via the "1-800" number reaches the desk of Whirlpool's director of product safety each morning. This daily monitoring enables him, and the company as a whole, to get on top of whatever potential issue has arisen just as soon as it comes to light. It enables Whirlpool to make judgments and act faster to protect consumers. Whirlpool makes every effort to intercept a product before it ever reaches the market by putting a hold on the model in question through the distribution system. In some cases, the product may have already reached consumers. In those situations, the extensive consumer data bank proves invaluable. Once the consumers who own the model in question are identified, Whirlpool relentlessly pursues them.
- Aim for early identification of problems. To make the product right and to make the owner feel comfortable and confident in its use, the earlier in the product's life a problem is identified, the easier it is to retrieve.
- Take corrective actions that eliminate the cause of the nonconformity.

- Implement process controls to prevent the cause of the potential nonconformities.
- Make permanent changes to procedures to prevent recurrence.
- Track open corrective actions to ensure timely closure.
- Ensure that corrective actions taken are effective. For example, an in-line sensor or mistake-proof device was added to an automated welding line as a result of a missing safety-related weld. A daily check was also instituted using a known "failure." The control plan was also revised to specify the daily check. As a verification measure, the responsible quality engineer checked the mistake-proof device's operation and the daily record prior to signing off on the corrective action report.

Typical Noncompliances in a Quality Systems Audit

- No preventive actions on four of five corrective actions reviewed.
- Control plan not revised to show increased monitoring.
- Past-due customer complaints show no evidence of corrective action.
- Cause not specified on two of nine corrective action reports.
- No evidence of corrective action follow-up to last internal audit noncompliances.

4.15 Handling, Storage, Packaging, Preservation, and Delivery

Establish and maintain procedures to ensure the preservation of quality product after manufacture.

Guidelines for Product Safety Programs

- Document and maintain procedures for all aspects of handling, through delivery.

- Specify safe handling methods to ensure product safety and quality. For example, the U.S. Food and Drug Administration requires food processors to follow Good Manufacturing Practices (GMPs). Certain protective equipment is required such as gloves and hair nets to prevent contamination. Storage and processing areas may require rodent control. In the case of milk and dairy products, Grade A refers to the level of sanitary processing standards. By necessity, the food industry focuses more on employee education and emphasizing that supervisors and workers be familiar with the principles of food protection.

- Specify methods for storage to prevent damage and deterioration.

- Document environmental conditions such as temperatures, humidity, cleanliness, lighting intensity, clean electrical power filters, fire protection, and any other required environmental parameters. For example, frozen foods need to be stored at all times below 32°F. Food poisoning bacteria multiplies above 32°F. Controls such as alarms, backup systems, and thaw alert sensors can be used to prevent spoilage. Storage may also apply as the product is in transit, for cold or freezer trucking.

- Specify responsibilities for packaging and marking processes. This area of product packaging failure is one of the high-ranking injury categories in the CPSC's NEISS database.

- Define clear responsibilities for package design and testing. Ensure that packaging instructions are available at all pack locations. For example, critical issues in food safety are tamperproof lids, expiration date coding, and cleanliness of food packages. The FDA has recognized issues with microwave packaging. Chemical components of adhesives, polymers, paper, and paperboard products used in microwave packaging migrate into food, but as yet the FDA has developed no regulations. This should throw up a warning flag to all microwave food producers relative to packaging safety and toxicity.

- Assess your stock areas, including chemical storage, to detect deterioration of raw, in-process, and finished products. For example, products such as food, drugs, inks, paints, and adhesives have a definite shelf-life. Many manufacturers require shelf-life labeling as a purchase order requirement. Typically, a shelf life or expiration date is found on the product's label. Other warnings, such as "do not freeze," may be included. Products that have exceeded their expiration date are in a state of deterioration, and should not be used for production purposes. Unfortunately, many lot dates are indecipherable unless you know how to crack the codes. Don't hesitate to call and ask the manufacturer.
- Specify safe methods for delivery and destination where contractually specified.
- Specify how late or short shipments will be handled. Your customer should be contacted for obvious reasons.

Typical Noncompliances in a Quality Systems Audit

- Tanker trucks used to haul food products were found to be lacking in cleaning procedures to purge all existing contents.
- Vacuum line packaging instruction not found, and obsolete instructions are on line, not marked as such.
- Five-gallon pail of resin found in stock ready to ship does not have a lock ring as specified in the packaging instruction.
- Antistatic band not worn by the operator as specified in the handling procedure.
- Out-of-date adhesive used in heat-shield assembly process; shelf life expired.
- Warning labels not placed on outgoing shipments of flammables.
- Temperature and humidity limits exceeded for proper test conditioning of samples.
- Improper date code applied to product at filler line.

Preventable Product Recalls Through Proper Handling, Storage, Packaging, Preservation and Delivery

- One of the leading brands of powdered milk was produced by a large food manufacturing company. Several years ago, a foodborne illness caused by salmonella was traced to this product. Adverse publicity caused the product to be withdrawn from the market and the brand name was retired.
- One company produced a line of canned gourmet foods until a foodborne illness outbreak related to clostridium botulinum was traced to one of its products. The negative publicity forced the company to go out of business.

4.16 Control of Quality Records

Procedures for identification, collection, storage, indexing, access, maintenance, and disposition of records.

Guidelines for Product Safety Programs

The purpose of the quality records element is to demonstrate your company's conformance to requirements and its effective operations in producing safe products. It also provides a strong liability prevention program, when it is done right. Quality records also provide input for corrective action and improvement. Records that show a committment to product quality and safety also may help your defense in product liability litigation.

Legal ramifications of keeping and disposing records categories must continue to be carefully evaluated on an ongoing basis. There are over 10,000 federal, state, and local statutes and regulations in the United States that govern specific record retention. No court will accept ignorance of a regulation as a satisfactory excuse for noncompliance. If your company is primarily regulated by a certain agency, it is good practice to obtain the titles of the federal regulations pertaining to your industry. For example, a food processing firm would be interested in Title 21, Food and Drugs.

A costly and perhaps flawed strategy of record retention is, "Let's keep everything forever. Then we are certain to be in compliance." This is a very costly way to achieve compliance. If the company is involved in litigation, it may result in having to produce everything it has relating to the suit. The records that are produced may not be in your company's best interest. Certain records are like a double-edged sword: In product liability litigation, a record can sometimes help, sometimes harm. For example, a memo questioning certain design aspects on a product could be detrimental, whereas documentation of a thorough design review and supporting data could prove to be very helpful.

It is legitimate to destroy a document in accordance with your retention program if you are not required to keep it. By implementing a consistent program for disposing of records, your company shows that it is not deliberately disposing of records to conceal evidence.

Many firms have a false sense of security because they have a disaster recovery plan for their computer systems. Unfortunately, resuming computer operations may not adequately protect older information that may be required for tax or legal reasons. A broader definition of vital records may need to be included in the disaster recovery plan. Off-site or duplicate storage may be considered. To get the maximum benefit it is important that only essential records be protected.

According to an American Records Management Association (ARMA) survey of companies implementing a records retention program for the first time:

- 24 percent of the total volume of records is disposed of when the program is begun.
- 32 percent of the records are sent to inactive storage.
- 43 percent of the active records remain in the office area, freeing half the space in the office once occupied by files.

QS-9000 specifies specific retention times and disposal times for records used in the automotive industry. For example, a combined list of records from ISO 9001, ISO 9004-1, and QS-9000 is shown in Table 5.1. It is not intended to be all inclusive. You will need to determine what records to keep based on your statutory, legal, regulatory, and customer requirements.

Table 5.1
Selected Combined List of Records from ISO 9001 and ISO 9004-1

Management reviews	Quality manual
Quality plans	Calibration records
Contract reviews	Test software verifications
Design reviews and validations	Corrective actions, internal and external
Specifications	Shipping and receiving records
Drawings	Sample submissions/ PPAP data
Regulations	Internal audits
Purchase orders and amendments	Training records
Approved supplier data	Service and warranty data
Traceability records	Customer complaints and incident reports
Inspect/test data	Electronic data and SPC charts
Equipment qualification/ maintenance	Statutory-specific records
Nonconforming disposition	Permits/regulatory
Repair, rework, scrap records	Tooling records
Test procedures	Quality cost data
Work instructions	Business plans
Operation procedures	

The list goes on, depending on your regulatory and legal requirements.

- Establish a record retention schedule that defines all specific types of records, retention times, and disposal of records. It is imperative that your company's legal counsel review and approve your record retention schedule. If the record retention schedule ever becomes a factor in litigation, one of the first issues that will be raised is whether the schedule had legal approval.
- Audit your records both for ISO 9000 and/or QS-9000 compliance, and for an effective liability prevention program.
- Prepare and maintain documented procedures that cover control of quality records. Store records, both paper and electronic, to prevent loss or damage. Make records available to customers, if required by contract.
- In summary:
  - — Inventory records
  - — Determine retention times
  - — Record the retention schedule
  - — Obtain approvals (both department heads and legal)
  - — Implement schedule of record retention

4.17 Internal Quality Audits

Set up a system of conducting audits of quality procedures and recommending and recording corrective actions.

Guidelines for Product Safety Programs

The internal audit function verifies your quality system's effective operations. The purpose of internal audits is to check to make sure your system is working to produce safe products and to meet customers' quality requirements. Each and every internal audit should answer three critical questions:

1. Are all detailed activities in the quality system carried out as intended?

2. Is the quality system effective in achieving the specified goals? (An overall parameter of effectiveness is customer complaints, based on customer satisfaction as a primary objective.)

3. Does the quality meet all external and customer requirements, including safety and regulatory requirements?

Additional guidance for auditing can be found in ISO 10011.

- Establish and maintain procedures for conducting internal audits.
- Develop an audit schedule that covers all functional departments within your company or all procedures within your quality system.
- Modify the schedule on the basis of the status of performance of the activity to be audited. Increase audit frequency for a poor performing area, or advance a scheduled date for a particular department if internal or external indicators warrant urgent actions.
- Use trained and qualified internal auditors that are independent of the area audited. For example, RAB accredited courses for lead assessors are helpful but not required. The ASQC refresher course and exam for certified quality auditor (CQA) s also highly recommended. It makes good business sense to send a few well chosen people to outside auditing training to develop their auditor skills.
- Include specific product liability verifications within your audit checklists, based on specific regulatory requirements.
- Record results of all internal audits and inform the persons responsible for the area audited. Make sure they understand each deficiency, as the corrective actions and response are due from that responsible department head, not from the internal auditor.

Avoid inflammatory language in audit reports, as they become a potential liability, or "smoking guns." It is important to write the findings in such a way that will not be misinterpreted later on. Just state the facts and avoid commentary. For example, phrases to avoid in audit reports include:

- Gross negligence
- Neglect
- Violation
- Reckless behavior
- Constitutes fraud
- Intentionally covered up safety hazards
- Situation could cause a hazard
- Facility is not in compliance with regulations

- The language should be factual: For example, rather than saying, "The facility does not have a records control program," the report might say, "No written procedure was found for records control."
- Sample size is also a very important issue to report. There is a big difference if a sample comes from one of one product (100 percent) or from one of 200 (0.5 percent).
- The audit results and subsequent corrective actions must be included in management review (4.1.3).
- Take prompt corrective action for all nonconforming findings, especially those that are safety-related. Companies may be convicted for failing to take corrective actions on safety items identified in their internal audits.
- Make thorough investigations into causes of noncompliances, and apply all steps as specified in element 4.14, Corrective and Preventive Action. Make changes to procedures and/or documentation resulting from systemic failure, or as deemed necessary to correct the problem.
- Scrutinize records in each audit, as they are the result of procedure and may serve as evidence for compliance and/or legal purposes. Selective sampling is an effective tool in systems audits.

The cross-functional matrix to help visualize cross-functional responsibilities is shown in Figure 5.7.

Typical Noncompliances in a Quality Systems Audit

- Internal audit found for assembly department; no corrective action response found for finding No. 3 (one of 16).
- Internal auditor used to audit engineering department is not independent of that function, as he or she reports to the vice president of engineering.
- Servicing functions done off-site not included in the internal audit function.

4.18 Training

Identify, carry out, and record all training needs of personnel.

Guidelines for Product Safety Programs

Many successfully registered companies consider training one of the most important elements in their quality program. In fact, the automotive supplement QS-9000 adds a section, "Training as a Strategic Issue," to this ISO element, and requires automotive suppliers to periodically evaluate training effectiveness.

Additional guidance on training and motivation can be found in ISO 9004-1.

- Document and maintain procedures to identify training needs, including minimum qualifications such as education, experience, and/or professional licensing.
- Document and maintain records of training for each employee.
- Develop training programs for various levels of the company, and budget for outside training based on historical usage and new proposed technologies. For example, a very important part of Whirlpool's proactive approach to safety

Figure 5.7
Cross-Functional Matrix by Department and Element of the Standard

#	Functional Matrix Summary	Mgt	Purch	Eng	QA	Lab	Sales	Mfg	HR	Maint	Inv/Ship	EHS
4.1	Management Responsibility	X										
4.2	Quality System	X		X	X		X					
4.3	Contract Review	X		X			X					
4.4	Design Control			X		X	X					
4.5	Document & Data Control	X	X	X	X	X	X	X	X	X	X	X
4.6	Purchasing		X									
4.7	Control of Customer-Supplied Product			X	X		X					
4.8	Product Identification & Traceability			X	X	X		X				
4.9	Process Control			X				X		X		X
4.10	Inspection & Testing				X	X		X				
4.11	Inspection, Measuring, & Test Equipment			X	X	X		X		X	X	
4.12	Inspection & Test Status				X	X		X				
4.13	Control of Nonconforming Product				X	X	X	X			X	
4.14	Corrective & Preventive Action	X	X	X	X	X	X	X				X
4.15	Handling, Storage, Packaging, & Delivery		X	X	X	X		X			X	
4.16	Control of Quality Records	X	X	X	X	X	X	X	X	X	X	X
4.17	Internal Quality Audits	X			X							X
4.18	Training	X							X			
4.19	Servicing						X					
4.20	Statistical Techniques			X	X	X		X				
	Customer Complaints	X		X	X		X					
***	**QS 9000 — Optional**											
11.1	Production Part Approval Process		X	X	X	X		X			X	
11.2	Continuous Improvement	X	X	X	X	X	X	X	X	X	X	X
11.3	Manufacturing Capabilities	X		X		X		X				

is its training and education program. Whirlpool has focused one aspect of training for product designers, developers, and marketers on product safety issues. Based on extensive analysis into the root causes of historic product failures, the company developed a required training program, which includes a series of detailed design checklists for every product in every product category manufactured.

- For example, the fire chief in Benton Harbor, Michigan, came to Whirlpool with some concerns following three mysterious home fires in the area. In each of the fires, clothes recently dried but removed from the dryer had suddenly ignited. There was no evidence of dryer involvement and none of the dryers were Whirlpool products. Whirlpool aggressively undertook a study targeted at finding the fires' origin. What the study indicated was that vegetable oil stains require cleaning with hot water and suds instead of warm water washes typically specified for today's fabrics, and that without that cleaning, fabrics soiled with oil catch fire if heated, whether in a hamper, by a dryer, or near a space heater. Whirlpool provided this information to allied industry groups and to the CPSC. The CPSC made a public warning to consumers. Whirlpool continues to warn dryer users with product labeling and literature.
- Provide appropriate technical training, not limited to the quality fields. Include functions such as sales, purchasing, maintenance, engineering, and product safety/regulatory staff.
- Identify individual training needs based on review of processes and update the training needs analysis.
- Determine how to train temporary agency workers and contractors.
- Establish methods for training staff who cannot read or speak English.
- Set up teams to train on new lines prior to start-up.
- Provide performance reviews to establish effectiveness of training.

- Corrective action for those employees that are not performing to expectations should include an evaluation of training needs.
- Document qualifications for trainers. They should know the process and how to teach.

Typical Noncompliances in a Quality Systems Audit

- Found six of ten new employees with no training record.
- Found three of nine engineers whose résumés and qualifications did not meet minimum qualifications of bachelor's degree in engineering plus five years of engineering experience.
- Found two of eight welders without Non-Destructive Testing certifications.
- No analysis or identification of training needs found.

4.19 Servicing

Establish and maintain documented procedures for ensuring that servicing is carried out in compliance with specifications.

Guidelines for Product Safety Programs

Document procedures for all on-site and off-site services your company performs. Include any warranty/repair, installation, and technical assistance functions. Many service applications have safety-related aspects. ISO 9004-1 provides additional guidance on servicing.

- Qualify any special tools or equipment for handling and servicing during or after installation. For example, at one facility, diagnostic equipment used to repair computer-assisted medical devices is qualified daily against several known failures, and a self-calibration routine is used prior to performing repair and diagnostics.
- Inspection and test equipment used in the field should be calibrated and controlled.

- Include instructions and up-to-date spare parts lists, along with any warnings to alert installers of potential risks. For example, static protection and spark-proof tools are required for gasoline pump installations, for obvious reasons. Multiple languages for assembly instructions and warnings may be required.
- Set up a toll-free line for technical service and/or spare parts. Make it simple for consumers to contact your service group and have up-to-date data regarding safety and product limitations. For example, Hewlett-Packard has various options for service contracts on its products. Numerous medical-device applications require arrangements for immediate replacement in case of failure. Hewlett-Packard's service options provide systems safety to consumers with urgent needs.
- Establish feedback and early warning systems to ensure rapid corrective actions for potential recalls.
- Include clear acceptance criteria for repairs, including any safety tests that are required.

4.20 Statistical Techniques

Identify and use appropriate statistical measurement techniques for assuring quality of product.

Guidelines for Product Safety Programs

Establish and maintain procedures for the selection and correct application of statistical tools for all processes within your organization. Although we list several specific techniques for product safety and liability prevention activities, there are many other methods and statistical tools available, which are beyond the scope of this book.

- Use statistical tools for the design process, such as reliability studies, safety evaluation and risk analysis, fault tree analysis, benchmarking, and failure mode and effects analysis.

- Use process control methods such as X-bar and r charts, Cpk and Ppk studies, P-charts, sampling plans, and pre-control.
- Use problem-solving tools such as Pareto analysis, cause-and-effect diagrams, correlation analysis, and confidence intervals.
- Use accuracy ratios and gage reliability and repeatability studies, and measurement uncertainty calculations for test and inspection equipment.
- Use collaborative testing, round robin, and blind samples for improving reliability of laboratory testing results.

Typical Noncompliances in a Quality Systems Audit

- Sampling plan is not followed in receiving inspection.
- SPC chart found on wave solder machine with out-of-control process point at 10:00 A.M. check; no notation made on the chart as to corrections made or containment.
- (QS-9000) Process Control Chart on the extruder (thickness) shows two out-of-control points, and there is no evidence of 100 percent inspection per the Ford ongoing process and product monitoring chart.

III

CONCLUSION

It is certainly possible to integrate product safety and workplace safety into your ISO 9000 or QS-9000 program. ISO 9000 and QS-9000 are not standards designed specifically for workplace safety and health—they are quality management system standards. Within the ISO or QS framework, however, an organization can realize such benefits as increased productivity and profitability through strategic alignment or integration of the ISO 9000 or QS-9000 effort with liability prevention and workplace safety programs. The two key points to remember are:

1. Product safety is a requirement of ISO 9001, ISO 9002, and QS-9000.
2. Workplace safety and health can be linked to your ISO 9000 or QS-9000 system for added value.

Global competition has forced many U.S. companies to cut costs and increase productivity. As a result, employees have acquired additional responsibilities. Although this is not news to you, remember that you can bring various management functions into harmony and thereby streamline these functions and reduce redundancies. For example, management systems, such as quality, product safety, environmental compliance, and workplace safety and health, can be combined or, at least, aligned. Some companies have already mastered this challenge by cutting out duplicated tasks in areas such as documentation, training, and auditing. They are cross-training employees at all levels to acknowledge the interrelationships among these functions. We hope that this book has opened new possibilities for your organization to explore in optimizing its compliance efforts.

III

APPENDIX A

SOURCES OF INFORMATION

Some Laws and Regulations That Affect Business:

Americans With Disabilities Act
Child Safety Protection Act
Comprehensive Environmental Response and Liability Act
Consumer Product Safety Act
EC and International Law
FDA Good Manufacturing Practices
Federal Boat Safety Act
Federal Coal Mine Health and Safety Act
Federal Food, Drug, and Cosmetic Act and Medical Device Statutes
Federal Hazardous Substances Act
Federal Metal and Nonmetallic Mine Safety Act
Federal Railroad Safety Act
Flammable Fabrics Act
Highway Safety Act
Magnuson-Moss Warranty Act
Occupational Safety and Health Act
Poison Prevention Packaging Act
Radiation Control Safety Act
Refrigerator Safety Act
Toxic Substances Control Act
Uniform Commercial Code

The preceding laws and regulations, along with many others, can be found in the *U.S. Federal Register*, and are available from your local library. The U.S. Department of Commerce also can help obtain foreign regulations and statutes.

Sources of Standards

American National Standards Institute (ANSI)
11 West 42nd Street
New York, NY 10036
Tel 212-642-4900 (General)
Fax 212-398-0023

American Society for Testing and Materials (ASTM)
100 Barr Harbor Drive
West Conshohocken, PA 19428-2959
Tel 610-832-9585
Fax 610-832-9555

National Fire Protection Association (NFPA)
1 Battery March Park
P.O. Box 9101
Quincy, MA 02269-9101
Tel 1-800-344-3555

The Chemical Manufacturers Association

The Chemical Manufacturers Association's Responsible Care® program is what the CMA refers to as the "Chemical Industry's contract with the public." The guiding principles of the program are:

- Recognize and respond to community concerns about chemicals and industry operations.
- Develop and produce chemicals that can be manufactured, transported, used, and disposed of safely.
- Make health, safety, and environmental considerations a priority in planning for all existing and new products and processes.
- Report promptly to officials, employees, customers, and the public information on chemical-related health or environmental hazards and recommend protective measures.
- Counsel customers on the safe use, transportation, and disposal of chemical products.
- Operate plants and facilities in a manner that protects the environment and the health and safety of employees and the public.

- Extend knowledge by conducting or supporting research on the health, safety, and environmental effects of chemical products, processes, and waste materials.
- Work with others to resolve problems created by past handling and disposal of hazardous substances.
- Participate with government and others in creating responsible laws, regulations, and standards to safeguard the community, workplace, and the environment.
- Promote the principles and practices of Responsible Care® by sharing expertise and offering assistance to others who produce, handle, use, transport, or dispose of chemicals.

Chemical Manufacturers Association (CMA)
Responsible Care® Department
1300 Wilson Boulevard
Arlington, VA 22209
Tel 703-741-5305

National Highway Transportation Safety Administration (NHTSA) U.S. Department of Transportation

Federal Motor Vehicle Safety Standards and Regulations (DOT HS 805 674, June 1989) are available from the U.S. Government Printing Office.

Other Sources of Information

American Industrial Hygiene Association (AIHA)
2700 Prosperity Avenue; Suite 250
Fairfax, VA 22031
Tel 703-849-8888
Fax 703-207-3561

American Society of Safety Engineers (ASSE)
1800 East Oakton Street
Des Plaines, IL 60018
Tel 847-692-4121

British Standards Institute (BSI)
389 Chiswick High Road
London W4 4AL
United Kingdom
0181 996 7002

Cal/OSHA Consultation Services
395 Oyster Point Boulevard
Room 325
South San Francisco, CA 94080
Tel 415-737-2843
California Guide to Developing Your Workplace Injury and Illness Prevention Program (SB 198)

National Council on Compensation Insurance
750 Park of Commerce Drive
Boca Raton, FL 33487
Tel 407-997-1000

National Safety Council
"Accident Facts"
1121 Spring Lake Drive
Itasca, IL 60143-3201
Tel 708-285-1315

United States Department of Labor
OSHA Information Office
Washington, DC 20210
Tel 202-606-6179

United States Consumer Product Safety Commission
Tel 1-800-638-2772

Product Certification Programs

Product certification programs, along with quality system registration programs, can help provide additional assurances for product safety, or at least a demonstration that care was taken in designing your product. Some examples of certification programs include:

Art and Creative Materials Institute Certification Program
Safety Equipment Institute
OSHA Nationally Recognized Testing Laboratory (Electrical)

Record Retention

Donald Skupsky. *Legal Requirements for Business Records: Information Requirements*. Englewood, CO: Information Requirements Clearing House (1994).

III

APPENDIX B

OSHA

Fact Sheet No. OSHA 9142 (September 1996)

Department of Labor, Occupational Safety and Health Administration, Regional Office

Region I (CT, MA, ME, NH, RI, VT)
John F. Kennedy Federal Building; Room E 340
Boston, MA 02203
Tel 617-565-9860

Region II (NJ, NY, PR, VI)
201 Varick Street; Room 670
New York, NY 10014
Tel 212-337-2378

Region III (DC, DE, MD, PA, VA, WV)
Gateway Building; Suite 2100
3535 Market Street
Philadelphia, PA 19104
Tel 215-596-1201

Region IV (AL, FL, GA, KY, MS, NC, SC, TN)
1375 Peachtree Street, N.E.; Suite 587
Atlanta, GA 30367
Tel 404-347-3573

Region V (IL, IN, MI, MN, OH, WI)
230 South Dearborn Street; Room 3244
Chicago, IL 60604
Tel 312-353-2220

Region VI (AR, LA, NM, OK, TX)
525 Griffin Street; Room 602
Dallas, TX 75202
Tel 214-767-4731

Region VII (IA, KS, MO, NE)
City Center Square
1100 Main Street; Suite 800
Kansas City, MO 64106
Tel 816-426-5861

Region VIII (CO, MT, ND, SD, UT, WY)
1999 Broadway; Suite 1690
Denver, CO 80202-5716
Tel 303-844-1600

Region IX (American Samoa, AZ, CA, Guam, HI, NV,
Trust Territories of the Pacific)
71 Stevenson Street; Room 415
San Francisco, CA 94105
Tel 415-975-4310

Region X (AK, ID, OR, WA)
James W. Lake, Regional Administrator
1111 Third Avenue; Suite 715
Seattle, WA 98101-3212
Tel 206-553-5930

The above states and territories operate their own OSHA-approved job safety and health programs (Connecticut and New York plans cover public employees only). States with approved programs must have a standard that is identical to, or at least as effective as, the federal standard.

Fact Sheet No. OSHA 9210 (1995)

The OSHA Voluntary Protection Program (VPP)

Program Highlights

Voluntary Protection Programs

Do you have an effective safety and health program? Is your injury and/or illness rate lower than the average for your industry? Do managers and employees work together to prevent accidents and eliminate hazards? Would you like to develop a more cooperative relationship with OSHA?

If so, your company may be a candidate for one of OSHA's Voluntary Protection Programs: Star, Merit, or the Demonstration Program. Designed to augment OSHA's enforcement efforts, these programs encourage and recognize excellence in occupational safety and health. Only those companies that demonstrate commitment to workplace safety and health beyond the requirements of the OSHA standards, especially at senior management levels, are eligible. Participation exempts a work site from OSHA's programmed inspections.

General Requirements

An effective, ongoing safety and health program. A strong safety and health program exemplifies commitment to the prevention of occupational illness and injury beyond satisfying the requirements of OSHA standards. It is the central element that qualifies a company for participation in the Voluntary Protection Programs. Companies participating in Merit and Star are expected to have comprehensive programs including elements such as employee participation and annual comprehensive self-evaluation. OSHA assesses the effectiveness of the program through a number of measures including on-site review.

Cooperation. A cooperative atmosphere is essential to make voluntary protection work. Construction companies are required to use a labor-management approach, which includes joint labor-management safety and health committees. General industry sites may use some other form of employee participation. Companies must demonstrate that the collective bargaining agent(s) representing their employees, if any, has (have) no objection to the company's participation. It is important under all Voluntary Protection Programs that both employers and employees recognize that they retain their rights and responsibilities under the Occupational Safety and Health Act.

Good performance. Although performance levels required vary with the individual Voluntary Protection Program, the company must demonstrate that its efforts are working to minimize injury and illness in the workplace. Two indicators are the Bureau of Labor Statistics injury incidence and lost workday injury rates. Also, the company must have demonstrated good faith in any previous dealings with OSHA.

Star

Open to any industry, Star is targeted for a company with comprehensive, successful safety and health programs. Companies that are in the forefront of employee protection as indicated by three-year average incidence and lost workday case rates at or below the national average for their industry may participate. They must also meet requirements for extensive management systems. Because of the changing nature of the work site, construction firms must maintain strong employee participation in their programs. Star participants are evaluated every three years, although their incident rates are reviewed annually.

Merit

Merit is an effective stepping-stone to Star. Merit sites may have more general management systems but must set goals for meeting Star requirements. Although there are less stringent rate requirements for Merit, applicants must agree to specific goals for reducing rates to below the average for their industry. Merit participants are evaluated on-site annually.

Demonstration

The Demonstration Program provides a basis for promising alternative safety and health program approaches that are not currently available under the VPP as well as to allow for special industry operations such as logging, maritime, etc. Alternative approaches that are successful will be considered for inclusion in the Star program.

OSHA Responsibilities

Application review. Each applicant undergoes a review of its safety and health programs including an on-site examination of its records and logs, a review of its inspection history, if any, and an assessment of site conditions. OSHA also conducts interviews of management and employees. The on-site portion of the review requires about four days.

Evaluation. Annual evaluations for Merit and Demonstration participants and three-year evaluations for Star participants compare injury and/or illness rates to industry rates, determine the satisfaction of participants, and assure that the companies continue to meet the requirements. In addition, at Merit sites, OSHA measures progress toward Star requirements.

Contact person. For each participant, OSHA provides a contact person to provide assistance.

Inspections. OSHA retains responsibility for inspections in response to formal, valid employee complaints, significant chemical leaks and spills, and workplace fatalities and catastrophes.

For applications or further information, write:

OSHA Voluntary Protection Programs
Room N3700
Frances Perkins DOL Building
200 Constitution Ave., NW
Washington, DC 20210
Tel 202-523-7266

Voluntary Safety and Health Program Management Guidelines:

The Occupational Safety and Health Administration (OSHA) has issued voluntary program management guidelines to encourage employers to do more than just comply with regulations to prevent occupational injuries and illnesses.

Although compliance with the law, including specific OSHA standards, is an important objective, an effective program looks beyond specific requirements of law to address all hazards. It seeks to prevent injuries and illnesses, whether or not compliance is at issue.

The language in these guidelines is general so that it may be broadly applied in general industry, shipyards, marine terminals, and longshoring activities regardless of the size, nature, or complexity of operations. Construction activities are not covered by this guideline because they are already covered under OSHA's construction standards.

The guidelines, a distillation of successfully applied safety and health management practices, are advocated by safety and health professionals and consultants representing corporations, professional associations, and labor unions.

The Guidelines

The guidelines call for systematic identification, evaluation, and prevention or control of general workplace hazards, specific job hazards, and potential hazards that may arise from foreseeable conditions.

The extent to which a program is described in writing is less important than how effective it is in practice. As the size of a work site or the complexity of a hazardous operation increases, however, the need for written guidance increases to ensure clear communication of policies and priorities and consistent and fair application of rules.

Major elements of an effective occupational safety and health program include:

Management Commitment and Employee Involvement. This calls for:

- A work site policy on safe and healthful work and working conditions clearly stated so that all personnel with responsibility at the site and personnel at other locations with responsibility for the site understand the priority of safety and health protection in relation to other organizational values.
- A clear goal for the safety and health program and objectives for meeting that goal so that all members of the organization understand the results desired and the measures planned for achieving them.

- Top management involvement in implementing the program so that all will understand that management's commitment is serious.
- Employee involvement in the structure and operation of the program and in decisions that affect their safety and health, to make full use of their insight and energy.
- Assignment of responsibilities for all aspects of the program, so that managers, supervisors, and employees in all parts of the organization know what performance is expected of them.
- Provision of adequate authority and resources to responsible parties, so that assigned responsibilities can be met.
- Holding managers, supervisors, and employees accountable for meeting their responsibilities, so that essential tasks will be performed.
- Annual reviews of program operations to evaluate their success in meeting the goal and objectives, so that deficiencies can be identified and the program and/or the objectives can be revised when the goal and objectives are not met.

Work-Site Analysis. This includes:

- Identification of all hazards by conducting baseline work-site surveys for safety and health and periodic comprehensive update surveys. Also included would be an analysis of planned and new facilities, processes, materials, and equipment, and another of routine job hazards.
- Regular site safety and health inspections, so that new or previously missed hazards and failures in hazard controls are identified.
- A reliable system to encourage employees, without fear of reprisal, to notify management personnel about conditions that appear hazardous and to receive timely and appropriate responses.
- Investigation of accidents and near-miss incidents, so that their causes and means for prevention are identified.
- Analysis of injury and illness trends over extended periods, so that patterns with common causes can be identified and prevented.

Hazard Prevention and Control. This calls for:

- Procedures that ensure that all current and potential hazards are corrected in a timely manner through engineering techniques where appropriate, and that safe work practices are understood and followed by all parties; provision of personal protective equipment; and administrative controls, such as reducing the duration of exposure.

Safety and Health Training. This includes training to:

- Ensure that all employees understand the hazards to which they may be exposed and how to prevent harm to themselves and others.
- Ensure that supervisors and managers understand their responsibilities and the reasons for them so they can carry out their responsibilities effectively.

III

APPENDIX C

INTERNET RESOURCE DIRECTORY

Much useful safety information is now located on the Internet, and more information is being added continuously. Any attempt to present a comprehensive listing of Internet information is by nature futile; the contents and addresses of sites change too rapidly. This directory therefore presents only a few main sites. Most of the information you need is either located on one of these sites, or may be found following links to other safety-related sites. The ES&H InfoCenter is a great place to start, presenting many resources previously found elsewhere, as well as providing links to other government sites.

ES&H InfoCenter
http://www.tis.eh.doe.gov/map.html

Combining technology and services, the Office of Information Management seeks to facilitate access to quality environmental, safety, and health information. Through the ES&H InfoCenter, an experienced research staff provides multimedia access to federal, industry, and international information sources. The Department of Energy's compilation of on-line information resources, as described on its Web site, is available by means of a point-and-click information map. Features available via this map include:

- ES&H Publications (Safety and Health bulletins, notes, and actions; NFS Safety Notices; and *Occupational Safety Observer*)

- ES&H TIS (Technical Information Services) Internet Resources Directory
- ES&H listing of conferences and training sessions
- OSHA Resources (Documents and Regulations, the *OSHA Technical Manual*, OSHA Standards, etc.)
- Regulatory Information (CFRs, the *Federal Register*, DOE Directives, Environmental Guidelines, and links to ANSI and ISO)
- Medical Information Links
- Environmental Information
- Chemical Safety Information (Chemical Substance Fact Sheets and Material Safety Data Sheets)
- Links to EPA, OSHA, Department of Defense, U.S. Nuclear Regulatory Commission, GILS (Government Information Locator Service), FedWorld, Canadian Centre for Occupational Health and Safety, among others.

Bureau of Labor Statistics News Release Data

gopher://pip.shsu.edu:70/11/Economics/bls
gopher://stats.bls.gov:70/1
ftp://ftp.shsu.edu/economics/bls/

The BLS news releases available on the Internet provide reports on the findings of several BLS programs along with national indicators such as the Employment Situation and the Consumer Price Index. The data includes Census of Fatal Occupational Injuries, Occupational Injuries and Illnesses (Annual), and Occupational Injuries and Illnesses by Selected Characteristics.

Consumer Product Safety Commission

http://www.cpsc.gov
gopher://cpsc.gov

On the Gopher site choose from:

Who We Are and What We Do for You
Chairman's Vision for CPSC
What's New at CPSC
Reporting Product Related Hazards to CPSC

CPSC Public Calendar
News from CPSC
CPSC Publications
Medical Examiners and Coroners Alert Project
Product Hazard Reports; Injury and Death Statistics
Federal Register Notices
CPSC Hotline Information
FY 93 - CPSC Annual Report
CPSC Information for Manufacturers, Retailers and Distributors
How to Receive Information from CPSC
To Automatically Receive Information from CPSC by E-Mail
Government Printing Office Access

The Web site contains the same information, although the organization differs.

Michigan State University Office of Radiation, Chemical, and Biological Safety

http://www.orcbs.msu.edu

Provides access to information on biological safety (e.g., biosafety policy, blood-borne pathogens, infectious diseases, hantavirus, medical waste, safety procedure, tuberculosis), chemical safety (e.g., hazardous materials table, hazardous waste manual, respirator program), radiation safety, materials safety data sheets (by material name and company name), newsletters, and links to other safety-related sites, among other useful tools.

III

APPENDIX D

CROSS-TABULATIONS OF STANDARDS

ISO 9001/ISO 14001

Figure D-1
ISO 9000/ VPP Cross-Tabulation

OSHA/VPP Guidelines for S&H

	4.1	4.2	4.3	4.4	4.5	4.6	4.7	4.8
	Mgmt	Qual	Ctrt	Desn	Doc	Prch	Cont	Prod
ISO 9001==>	Resp	Syst	Rev	Ctrl	Ctrl		Cust	Trac
OSHA VPP								
1 i Policy	X							
1 ii Communicate Golas & Objectives		X						
1 iii Top Management Involvement	X							
1 iv Employee Involvement								
1 v Assign Responsibility	X							
1 vi Provide resources	X							
1 vii Hold accountable	X							
1 viii Review results		X						
2 i Analysis		X						
2 i A Baseline survey		X						
2 i B Analyze planned processes			X	X		X		
2 i C Perform routine analyses								
2 ii Periodic inspections								
2 iii Employee concern system								
2 iv Accident Investigation								
2 v Analyze trends		X	X					
3 Hazard Prevention and Control				X				
3 i A Engineering techniques				X				
3 i B Training & Enforcement	X							
3 i C PPE provided								
3 i D Administrative Controls	X	X					X	X
3 ii Maintenance								
3 iii Emergency Preparedness	X							
3 iv Medical program	X	X						
4 Training								
4 i Employee training								
4 ii A Supervisor Hazard analysis	X							
4 ii B Super Maintenance of workplace	X							
4 ii C Super Reinforce employee training	X							
4 iii Ensure managers understand responsibility	X							

4.9	4.10	4.11	4.12	4.13	4.14	4.15	4.16	4.17	4.18	4.19	4.20
Proc	Insp	Ctrl	Insp	Ctrl	Corr	Hand	Rec	Int	Trng	Serv	Stat
Ctrl	Test	Eqpt	Stat	Nonc	Actn	Stor	Ctrl	Audt			
								X			
	X	X	X								
	X	X	X								
					X						
					X						
					X						
									X		
									X		
									X		
									X		
		X	X								
									X		
					X				X		
									X		
									X		
X									X		
X									X		
									X		
									X		

Figure D-2
Links Between ISO 14000 and ISO 9000

ISO 9001: 1994 Element \ ISO 14000: 1996 Element	4.0 General	4.1 Environmental Policy	4.2 Planning	4.2.1 Environmental Aspects	4.2.2 Legal	4.2.3 Objectives/Targets	4.2.4 Env. Mgt. Program	4.3.1 Structure and Responsibility	4.3.2 Training	4.3.3 Communication	4.3.4 EMS Documentation	4.3.5 Document Control	4.3.6 Operational Control	4.3.7 Emergency Preparedness	4.4.1 Monitoring	4.4.2 NonConform & Cor. Action	4.4.3 Records	4.4.4 EMS Audit	4.5 Management Review
4.1 Management Responsibility	X	X		X		X	X	X											X
4.2 Quality System	X										X		X						
4.3 Contract Review													X						
4.4 Design Control													X						
4.5 Document & Control Data												X							
4.6 Purchasing													X						
4.7 Control of Customer Supplied Product													X						
4.8 Product ID and Traceability																			
4.9 Process Control													X						
4.10 Inspection & Testing															X				
4.11 Control of Inspection, Measuring & Test Equipment															X				
4.12 Inspection and Test Status																			
4.13 Control of NonConforming Products																X			
4.14 Corrective and Preventive Action														X		X			
4.15 Handling, Storage, Packaging, etc.													X						
4.16 Control of Quality Records																	X		
4.17 Internal Quality Audits																		X	
4.18 Training									X										
4.19 Servicing													X						
4.20 Statistical Techniques																			

Note: Cell with an X denotes a link.

Figure D-3
ISO 9000 Key Word Matrix

	ISO 9001	QS-9000	ISO 9004-1	ISO 9004-2	ISO 9004-3
KEYWORD	CLAUSE/ ELEMENT	CLAUSE/ ELEMENT	CLAUSE/ ELEMENT	CLAUSE/ ELEMENT	CLAUSE/ ELEMENT
SAFETY		4.2.3a	8.4.2a5	4.1	4.3.1
		4.6.1	14.4, 14.6	6.1.1	7.2c
		4.6.3	15.3	6.1.4	8.2.4
		4.9b	16.3, 16.6	6.2.4.3	8.2.5
		4.9d	18.2		8.5.2c4
			19		15.3, 15.8
			20.1h		19
REGULATORY/	4.4.4	4.4.4	8.4.2a6	6.1.2	7.2d
STATUTORY		4.9d			12.3g
		4.9b			
ENVIRONMENT	4.9b	4.17	8.4.2a5	5.2.3	5.5c
			10.3	5.3.2.1	7.2c
			17.2	6.1.1	10.1.1, 10.3
				6.1.4	17.3
					19
RISK	4.14	4.14	8.8		8.4, 14.2, 19
HEALTH				6.1.1, 6.1.4	

III

APPENDIX E

FURTHER READING

Allen, Mike. "May the Cornering Force Be With You." *Popular Mechanics.* December 1995.

ASQC Chemical and Process Industries Committee. *ANSI/ASQC Q90/ISO 9000 Guidelines for Use by the Chemical and Process Industries.* Milwaukee, WI: ASQC Quality Press (1992).

Beauregard, Michael, Raymond Mikulak, and Robin McDermott. *The Basics of Mistake-Proofing.* New York: Quality Resources (1997).

CEEM. *ISO 9000 Registered Company Directory.* Burr Ridge, IL: CEEM (1995).

Chynoweth, Emma. "Opening the ISO 9000 Umbrella to Cover Health, Safety, and the Environment." *Chemical Week.* November 10, 1993.

Cooper, Robert. *Winning At New Products.* 2nd ed. Reading, MA: Addison-Wesley (1993).

Diamond, Susan. *Records Management.* 3rd ed. New York: AMA-COM (1995).

Dutch Council for Certification (Stichting Raad Voor De Accreditatie; RvA). 1994 Annual Report.

Dyjack, David and Steven Levine. "Development of an ISO 9000 Compatible Occupational Health Standard: Defining the Issues." *American Industrial Hygiene Association Journal.* June 1995.

Freeman, Harry. *Industrial Pollution Prevention Handbook.* New York: McGraw-Hill (1995).

Green, Mark. *The Consumer's Bible.* New York: Workman Publishing (1994).

Greeno, J. Ladd, G. S. Hedstrom, and M. Di Berto. *Environmental Auditing.* 2nd ed. Cambridge, MA: Arthur D. Little (1985).

Hale, Judith A. and Odin Westgaard. *Achieving a Leadership Role for Training.* New York: Quality Resources (1995).

Hammer, Willie. *Product Safety.* Des Plaines, IL: ASSE (1994).

ISO. *AIAG Quality System Requirements QS-9000.* 2nd ed. Detroit, MI: Automobile Industry Action Group (1995).

ISO. *ISO 9000 Compendium.* 4th ed. Geneva: ISO (1994).

Juran, J. M. *Juran's Quality Control Handbook.* 4th ed. New York: McGraw-Hill (1988).

Kolb, John and S. S. Ross. *Product Safety and Liability.* New York: McGraw-Hill (1989).

Kolka, James and G. G. Scott. *European Community Product Liability and Product Safety Directives.* Burr Ridge, IL: CEEM (1992).

Kozak, Bob and Rick Clements. "ISO 9000 and Work Safety." *Quality Digest.* May 1995.

Kume, Hitoshi. *Management by Quality.* New York: Quality Resources (1995).

Lack, Richard W., ed. *Essentials of Safety and Health Management.* Boca Raton, FL: Lewis Publishers (1996).

Liebowitz, Alan J., ed. *Industrial Hygiene Auditing: A Manual for Practice.* Fairfax, VA: American Industrial Hygiene Association Publications (1994).

Mansdorf, S. Z. *Complete Manual of Industrial Safety.* New York: Prentice Hall Law and Business (1993).

Marriott, N. *Principles of Food Sanitation.* 3rd ed. New York: Chapman & Hall (1995).

McArthur, C. Dan and Larry Womack. *Outcome Management.* New York: Quality Resources (1995).

McDermott, Robin, Raymond Mikulak, and Michael Beauregard. *The Basics of FMEA.* New York: Quality Resources (1996).

Murphy, Anne. "Entrepreneur of the Year, Allen Breed." *Inc. Magazine.* December 1995.

National Highway Traffic Safety Administration. *Draft Strategic Plan.* October 1995.

Niland, Jill, ed. *Accident Prevention Manual for Business and Industry, Volume 1: Administration and Programs.* 11th ed. Itasca, IL: National Safety Council (1997).

Peach, Robert, ed. *The ISO 9000 Handbook.* 2nd ed. Burr Ridge, IL: CEEM (1994).

Rabbitt, John T. and Peter A. Bergh. *The Miniguide to QS-9000.* New York: Quality Resources (1996).

Shingo, Shigeo. *Poka Yoke: The Shingo Production Management System.* Portland, ME: Productivity Press (1992).

Smith, S. L. "IBM Spells Safety 'ISO.'" *Occupational Hazards.* December 1995.

Steinman, D. and S. Epstein. *The Safe Shopper's Bible.* Old Tappan, NJ: Macmillan (1995).

Stone, James R., Jr. "How to Avoid Explosions at Airbag Plants." *Business Week.* January 22, 1996.

Struebing, Laura. "9000 Standards?" *Quality Progress.* January 1996.

"Taurus Wins." *Insurance Institute for Highway Safety Status Report.* December 1995.

United States Consumer Product Safety Commission. *Regulatory Reform Initiative Summary Report.* Bethesda, MD: USCPSC. June 1995.

United States Government, Office of the Federal Register. Consumer Product Safety Act Regulations. Code of Federal Regulations 16 Part 1100 to 1406. Washington, DC: U.S. Government Printing Office. 1995.

III

INDEX